HEALING THE
Shadow

DEEP PROCESS PSYCHOTHERAPY

MARIANNE HILL

An invitation into the transformational world of SHADOW WORK

First published by Healing The Shadow, August 2024

ISBN 978-1-0687245-0-3 (paperback)
ISBN 978-1-0687245-1-0 (ebook)

Cover design Rachel Kelli

This book is dedicated to my partner, Neil,
who taught me the simplicity of love.

Acknowledgements

I would like to acknowledge all the teachers and mentors I have had over the years who have shown me how to lead with authenticity, humility and heart, and who have put love at the centre of their practice. In particular I would like to thank Keith Phillips, Clive Busby, Nigel Felton and Dominique Sakoilsky.

I would also like to offer special thanks to those who supported me in the writing of this book: Rosemary Whaley, Freya Randall, Barnaby King, Karen Noonan and Neil Croom. Your feedback has been invaluable.

Contents

PART THREE

Foreword

Change seems to be happening all over the world, with old certainties crumbling, and a sense of new structures emerging. Perhaps because of this, or perhaps because the time was right anyway, therapy too seems to be maturing into something more human, more compassionate perhaps, and certainly more effective. For many decades in the past therapy rested on a relationship of superiority – one in which the therapist regarded the client as someone to be treated, cured or changed. In *Healing The Shadow*, my colleague Marianne Hill has created a therapeutic system where the client is in control of their own process, and which is founded on a relationship of safety, respect and equality. Healing The Shadow practitioners see their clients as people who hold the answers to their own challenges, people who only need the support of their practitioner in finding their own way back to the truth of who they always were, before, as I like to imagine, 'the world got in the way'. With that principle as their foundation stone, practitioners are empowered to sit alongside their clients and watch the grace of human potential unfolding in the room before them. I feel privileged to have played a part in the evolution of Healing The Shadow into a new approach to emotional healing, and more privileged still to have been involved with the training of a new generation of practitioners who will take the philosophy, skills and techniques of this exciting new way of healing out into the world. For all of this, and for the abundant joy and humanity she brings to her work, I am grateful to Marianne.

Rod Boothroyd, author of *Warrior, Magician, Lover, King*

Introduction

Imagine for a moment a therapy session where you have the time and space to relax deeply into the process, and to fully experience what is going on inside. Imagine being able to lay out your inner world in front of you so that you can really see what's happening there, and then imagine being able to explore and express all these different parts of yourself in an embodied and experiential way. Imagine what it might be like for you to be the one in control of the pace, the content and the direction of this work, and finally, imagine being able to step into your inner world and bring about the changes you wish to see there in order to create profound and lasting change to your everyday life.

Well, this is no imaginary world – this is the world of Healing The Shadow, and this book describes such sessions and the theory and beliefs behind the work that I teach and practise.

The story of Healing The Shadow

The journey to creating Healing The Shadow started over a quarter of a century ago in 1998, when I first found myself drawn to exploring personal development work. Simply put, I knew I needed support. I was facing an extremely challenging time in my life. My relationship had ended, I felt alone in the world and was overwhelmed with many difficult emotions which, unbeknownst to me at the time, had their roots in unprocessed childhood trauma. I was also facing the very real everyday problems of being a single parent, and the stresses and strains of working as a physics teacher in an inner-city school.

During that time I tried many different types of counselling and psychotherapy, yet I was never able to find something which offered me the space, time and depth of connection I felt I needed. I now know I wasn't alone in looking for a more nourishing experience. Many people have since told me of their need for something beyond traditional talking therapies that would meet them in a deeper and more embodied way. However, at the time I didn't have the language to express what I was searching for and I had limited success in finding a therapy that really worked for me.

Despite never coming across quite the right approach, I found my interest in personal development work persisted, and over time I came to know that I wanted to study and practise therapeutic work myself. It wasn't a thought as such; there was no moment when I realised this was what I wanted to do. It felt more like something that was clear and innate within me, something that had always been there but was only now becoming apparent. As this knowledge revealed itself, I began to explore the possibility of training in psychotherapy.

Given my financial limitations at the time, it wasn't possible for me to undertake conventional psychotherapy training; it was simply out of my reach, and it seemed as though my journey would come to an end before it had even begun. However, browsing a local newspaper one day I came across Relate, an organisation in the UK that works with couples, families and individuals. They had a policy of providing free training whilst their trainees worked with clients, unpaid, throughout the training process and beyond. This suited me perfectly, allowing me to undertake a therapeutic training whilst at the same time gaining valuable experience. I couldn't believe my luck in having stumbled upon a solution to what had seemed, up until then, to be an insurmountable problem. I will never forget the excitement of receiving the call telling me that I had been accepted on their training programme.

Through practising couples work, I came to understand the hidden connections that play out in intimate and family relationships, and the wounds that bind people into dances which unfold without their knowledge or awareness. It was beautiful to work with couples and make this unconscious process conscious so that they could begin to work together to heal the wounds they carried. This was where I first came across the concept of the shadow, and where I witnessed first-hand the impact that unprocessed shadow material can have on relationships. I also saw the transformation that is possible when couples come together to support each other in their growth, rather than allowing their painful patterns of behaviour to play out in destructive ways.

Although I hadn't set out to study couples work, I came to see how essential relationship work is to our healing as individuals. I now believe that an understanding of what happens in relationships is necessary for *any* therapist, whether working with individuals or couples. Consequently, studying relationship dynamics and effective communication is an integral part of the work we do at Healing The Shadow, and I am so grateful that, entirely by accident, my first experience of therapeutic work was in the field of relationships.

As I became more experienced in relationship work, I started to look for further training which focused specifically on my own personal development and the role this played in my client work. I had a strong sense that this was a missing piece for me that could enrich what I offered. Coincidentally, I was on a simultaneous journey in my personal life, looking for ways of relaxing that would support me in facing the challenges I was experiencing at that time. I was searching for ways to have more control over my internal world and to experience greater peace in my body and mind. Through this exploration, I came across shiatsu, and I found that this ancient form of bodywork brought about a profound sense of healing and relaxation within me; it was clearly working on emotional and psychological levels, as well as the physical.

Inspired, I went on to train with the Bristol School of Shiatsu, where there was a strong focus on each individual trainee's personal growth and development. This was just the type of further training I had been searching for, but I hadn't expected to find it in the field of bodywork. Again, my journey took me away from my expected path in a most delightful way.

In training in shiatsu, a new world opened up for me. We were taught about how, when touching the client, we were energetically in touch with the whole of their being, and in a similar way the client was connected to everything that was going on inside us as we worked with them. This meant that, as practitioners, we needed to work with our own thoughts and feelings whilst we were in contact with the client, and to find a way to hold and process these and allow them to flow. If our emotions were repressed or stuck, we were told, we might block the flow of energy in the client, limiting the healing which might be possible for them.

Through this understanding, my own wellbeing became intertwined with my practice in a beautiful way, and I saw this idea was true whether or not I was working in physical connection with my client. Indeed, I saw that whatever form of therapeutic work we practise, our internal state and our own wellbeing play a significant role in the healing that is possible for the client. This was the missing piece I had been looking for.

Through my study at the Bristol School of Shiatsu, I began to understand how our bodies store unprocessed trauma: emotions we have not yet been able to feel. These show up in many ways, including aches, pains, illnesses and body posture. I learnt how to listen in depth to another person's body and being and to start to speak the language of the body, supporting people to come to know and listen to the wisdom they hold within them. Round about this time I also came across the work of David Grove, who showed us how the body communicates with us through imagery and metaphors and how to use these metaphors to support us in resolving traumatic memories.

David Grove's work further stimulated my interest in using body wisdom as a pathway to healing, and I began to explore how I could bring these new ideas into my therapeutic practice. In supporting clients to listen to their bodies, I found I was able to deepen the work I offered. The information their bodies revealed pointed us towards the hidden roots of the difficulties they were experiencing, and paying attention to these newly discovered aspects of the client allowed for more full-bodied and integrated change to take place.

As my interest in embodied practices grew, I came across a style of working that was to have a profound impact on my life, both personally and professionally. A fellow shiatsu student introduced me to a dream therapist by the name of Clive Busby, and with him I explored the power of stepping into different parts of my psyche and allowing these to speak. The depth of this embodied 'parts work' took my breath away. Clive was particularly skilled at working with the wounded child parts of me that needed such care and attention, and I did much of my early healing work under his guidance. Deeply impressed by the transformational nature of this way of working, I began to weave both parts work and Inner Child work into my own practice. This added a completely new dimension, bringing greater potency and vitality to my work and allowing clients to work at depth whilst still having full control over the parts of themselves they explored and how deep they wished to go.

At the same time, shadow work was becoming a hot topic at the Bristol School of Shiatsu. Our teachers explained how parts of us can be hidden away and stored in our bodies, where they can affect our lives in unconscious ways. It seemed clear to me that shadow work and body work were intrinsically linked, and I began to explore shadow work for my own personal healing. I was deeply moved by the experience of being witnessed and compassionately held and met in my darkest and most unspoken and unseen places.

I intuitively knew this work was where my future lay, and by this time I was resourced enough, both practically and financially, to be able to train in shadow work with an organisation based in the United States, called Shadow Work Seminars, Inc. Through their training, I learnt an incredibly powerful system for working with the shadow, developed by their founder, Cliff Barry. This is where I came across deep process work for the first time and learnt how we can consciously and deliberately intervene to change the powerful dynamics that rule our lives. I integrated this work into the work I was already practising and, over the years that followed, I developed a way of working with clients based on these combined modalities. Finally I had the therapy I had so longed for nearly twenty years before! As my work became more popular, I was able to leave my school teaching role and focus full-time on my therapeutic practice.

Looking back now, it was an incredible stroke of luck for me that I was unable to take the conventional psychotherapy training route. Instead my journey took me down a completely different path, which led me to the work I practise today, and for that I am extremely grateful.

In 2018 I founded Healing The Shadow, an organisation offering healing work for individuals, couples and groups. This is when Rod Boothroyd joined me and we began running group Healing The Shadow journeys together. As well as being trained in shadow work, Rod brought his own wealth of experience from the worlds of archetypal therapy and transactional analysis. Joining forces with Rod, the work I did went deeper, and we continued to develop the Healing The Shadow model together.

After experiencing profound change in their own lives, a number of our clients began to enquire about the possibility of training with us. We saw the need and decided to offer our own professional training course in the style of work we'd developed together. We both clearly remember the landmark moment when, sitting together in a cafe in Totnes, we started to plan a possible syllabus for our training. We were so excited to start this process, to really structure our ideas about the work we were doing and how we might pass this on to others. Within a very short time, really, from that initial meeting, we had developed our intensive two-year training programme in Deep Process Psychotherapy. With Rod's mentorship and support, I have been running this training ever since, and we now have a vibrant community of qualified practitioners offering this work across the UK.

Why Deep Process Psychotherapy?

It is only recently that we settled on the term 'Deep Process Psychotherapy' as a way to describe our work. Initially we had resistance to using the term 'psychotherapy', as this work is so radically different from traditional forms of therapy, both in its underlying philosophy and in the way the sessions are structured. However, we also wanted to claim the word psychotherapy for ourselves as a way of conveying the depth, breadth, quality and professionalism of the work we do. So eventually we settled on Deep Process Psychotherapy.

If we break the word psychotherapy down, we have two parts: firstly 'psyche', which is derived from the Greek word for soul, and secondly 'therapy', with its roots in the Greek word for healing. So at its core psychotherapy could be seen as describing 'healing of the soul', a term which we find beautifully expresses the nature of the work we do. At the same time, we use the phrase 'deep process' to set us apart from traditional psychotherapy by indicating the embodied and process-orientated nature of the work.

An invitation into the world of Healing The Shadow

My aim is that in reading this book you will immerse yourself fully in the world of Healing The Shadow and come to understand the heart and essence of this transformative work. Through stories of fictional clients and their sessions, you will be introduced to shadow work, embodied parts work and process work. You will also learn about the principle of wholeness that is at the core of our practice, and the archetypal theory that shapes the framework we use. Through the lens of this accessible and engaging framework, you will be able to explore your own wounds and life challenges, gaining insight into the shadows you may carry and what your personal pathway to healing might be.

Before you read this book

Before you read this book, I would like to draw your attention to a few important points.

Firstly, this is NOT a training manual. To practise this work with clients requires a high level of specialised intensive training and years of personal experience of working with your own shadow. Please do not try any of the processes described in this book without undertaking the appropriate training. It would not be safe to do so.

Secondly, many of the ideas and processes described in this book are explained via the stories of fictional characters. It is important to be clear that these characters and their stories are entirely imaginary and are not based on any of my clients nor on anyone else I have met or heard of.

Thirdly, this is not an exercise book. The book is designed to give a flavour of the work we do but is not designed as a way for you to do your own shadow work, nor is it a replacement for therapy sessions.

Fourthly, a note on the use of the terms 'therapist' and 'practitioner'. In Healing The Shadow we tend to call ourselves practitioners rather than therapists. Through the book I have used the term 'practitioner' to refer to Healing The Shadow practitioners only, and 'therapist' to refer to the wider profession.

Finally, I have restricted myself to explaining only the Healing The Shadow concepts and processes that are *different* from those used in traditional psychotherapy. There are many overlaps between our work and traditional psychotherapy, so throughout the book I also touch on some important psychotherapeutic principles that are widely used by many therapists. I don't, however, describe these in detail, as they have been extensively written about elsewhere, so if you are new to these ideas I invite you to explore them further via your own reading. I have included a list of suggested reading at the end of the book.

Please note: this book does not cover the relationship work I teach – the Five Fields framework, the Restoring Connection process and client/practitioner dynamics. These may be the subject of a future book.

Part One

1.

Embodied Parts Work

The room is completely silent. The practitioner, Sam, is leaning forwards, eager to hear any sound that emerges from his client Joe, who is curled into a tight ball on the floor, wrapped in a pale blue cloth. Joe is completely still. The moment extends.

After several minutes Joe makes an almost imperceptible movement with his head, very slightly turning it towards his practitioner. Sam takes his cue and asks Joe what is happening for him. 'I feel so small,' Joe says, in the tiniest whisper. 'I can hardly speak; I can hardly move. I am so frightened.' There is a long pause... 'I am hiding.'

Welcome to the world of shadow work.

Here, Joe is in the middle of a session with Sam, and he is exploring some of the challenges he is facing in his workplace. He has chosen to step into the part of himself that lacks confidence at work. This has turned out to be a very small and frightened part of him, which Sam is speaking to with great care and sensitivity.

To explore parts in Healing The Shadow, we use a carpet in the centre of the room to represent the client's inner world. When a client wishes to explore a part of themselves, they choose a coloured cloth to represent that part – all practitioners have a good mix of large coloured cloths in their practice rooms. The client then steps onto the carpet and decides where this part of them lives in their inner world. Joe has chosen the furthest left-hand corner of the carpet for the part he is exploring.

The client is then invited to go to that place on the carpet, to wrap the coloured cloth around themselves and to allow themselves to completely become that part. They take on the posture, the thoughts and the feelings of that part, and they speak to the practitioner *from* that part. This is a very different experience from speaking *about* the part and describing it to the practitioner. The part now comes alive in the client's body and mind. They temporarily become that part of themselves and they feel and speak as if they were that part.

When exploring parts in this way, we enter the hidden world of the client's inner landscape. When the client gives themselves permission to completely inhabit a part of themselves, we discover the 'essence' of that part. The client finds themselves speaking things they didn't even know they thought or felt. They may be so used to trying to push that part away, or to sanitise it and make it presentable, that they have never really met that side of themselves properly and got to know it.

Stepping into parts in this way is the cornerstone of the work we do. These parts may be loud, angry, mean, aggressive, quiet, shy, scared, timid or anything in between. By inhabiting these parts and having them seen and accepted by our practitioner, we can find out more about these sides of ourselves and come to know ourselves more fully.

You may now be thinking there is good reason why most therapists *don't* practise in this way! Do we, as therapists, *really* want to meet mean or vindictive parts of our clients, or parts that hate therapists, for example, or that hate people of our gender or background? What about parts that don't want to live, or parts that have no boundaries?

A deep capacity for holding is required in a practitioner if they are to meet such parts. Ultimately the practitioner must have reached a point of knowing that they *themselves* have such parts within them, and that it has been safe to explore these parts. If we are not afraid of painful or destructive parts of ourselves, then we will find we are not afraid of the painful or destructive sides of our clients.

One of our core principles in Healing The Shadow is that *all* parts of every person are welcome in the room. We understand they are there for a reason. They have a role to play, and they are serving the client in some way. We see the goodness in all parts of each person.

When we're working with the shadow, we hold the belief that true joy comes from knowing, accepting and loving *all* parts of ourselves. This means knowing and accepting the parts of us that are in deep grief or filled with rage, frightened, hesitant, vindictive, hateful or full of shame or guilt. It means welcoming these parts into our conscious realm, having them witnessed and understood by others, and tenderly caring for them and listening to their needs and the powerful emotions they carry. As we come to know and accept more and more of ourselves, we find we are more able to sit back, relaxed in our own skin, knowing there is nothing in us that we fear and nothing we need to hide. Sitting in this place colours all our life experiences. It gives us a deep self-assurance, no matter what is happening around us, and allows joy to arise even in the midst of life's most difficult challenges. We lead ourselves through life from a foundation of confidence, which comes from knowing and trusting ourselves with all our varied and complex parts, and coming to love and accept the person we truly are.

This position we hold can only genuinely be reached when a practitioner has completed enough of their own shadow work to know and understand it is true from their own experience. This happens when they have been through the process of coming to know and accept parts of themselves they had previously believed were shameful, unacceptable or dangerous, when they have come to understand the motivation of those parts and the value they hold, and they are no longer frightened or disturbed by these parts of themselves. Although this process of accepting and owning shadow parts continues throughout a person's whole lifetime, to have had experience of owning and accepting *some* parts of ourselves engenders confidence and trust that this process is possible, both for us and for our clients.

Another important principle of our work is that parts can only really do harm when they are pushed away and denied. They then come out by accident, against our will. They burst out in uncontrolled ways and can wreak havoc in our lives. In our daily lives we act unconsciously from these parts. In a Healing The Shadow session the very act of deliberately and consciously stepping into a part takes this unconscious element out of the equation. We find that when parts are inhabited consciously, there is always a part of the client that is still in control and, for example, will not allow that part to break anything, or leave the room, or behave in a way that would sabotage their healing.

Because the client has stepped consciously into the part, they are in control of that part and can step consciously *out* of it when they or the practitioner might need them to.

The concept of parts is also very helpful in lifting shame from the client. For example, if a client believes they are a selfish person, they can experience intense shame about this and not want to admit that they are selfish or to explore it further. However, if they see that they have a selfish *part* of them, then this is easier to accept. They can understand this is just a part of them and they are also made up of many other parts. The selfishness is *not* the whole of them. They know that once they have finished exploring that part, they can step out of the cloth and back into their full self. In this way parts work allows clients to look at previously unexplored parts of themselves in a safe way, knowing these are only a part of them and not the whole story of who they are.

As described earlier, when clients step fully into a part of themselves, they can discover previously unexpressed thoughts and feelings. It's as though their body memory kicks in. Images, recollections, thoughts and feelings emerge, often from way back in the client's life. This can give insight into the root of a particular trauma or a particular behaviour or thought pattern.

If we go back to Joe on the carpet in his blue cloth, who has just told us he is hiding, the next question Sam asks him, in a very gentle voice, is 'How old are you feeling?' Joe whispers back, 'I feel about three. I am under the stairs. It's so dark. I am so alone. I want to scream out, but I can't. I'm frightened.'

We now have information about the early roots of the feelings Joe carries inside him. Joe has never been able to understand why these feelings emerge in the workplace and destroy his confidence. He and Sam now have some insight into what he is having to face each day as he goes into work and these three-year-old feelings arise inside him.

Sam continues to talk to little Joe about what he is thinking and feeling. We find that mostly clients enjoy being in these kind of child parts, as the child is now getting some care and attention in a situation where they previously had none. However, we always make sure the client knows they can step out of the part at any time if it gets overwhelming. They can simply take off the cloth they are wearing, put it down on the carpet and come back to their seat opposite the practitioner.

This has the powerful effect of the client being able to 'leave' the feelings of that part on the carpet and step back into the whole of themselves. It is an important safety mechanism in the work that we do.

This can also be a very empowering experience for the client. For many people this is the first time they will have experienced the conscious choice of stepping out of an overwhelming emotional state and back into their full adult self.

In my early days as a client of parts work, I stepped regularly into an eleven-year-old part of myself. As this young girl talked with my practitioner, a pain would develop in my left shoulder. This would become more and more intense the longer the young girl spoke. Eventually the pain would become too much for me and I would step out of the part and back into my chair. The pain then immediately left my shoulder.

This is a good example of the conscious choice clients have as to how much they wish to experience certain parts of themselves and how they can keep themselves safe by stepping out of parts whenever they wish.

So, as mentioned before, when the client wants to step out of a part, they leave the cloth on the carpet where they have been standing or sitting. They then arrange the cloth in a way that represents that part of themselves, and they can also choose one of the objects from around the room to bring that part to life a bit more so that it is represented accurately for them on the carpet. For example, if they have been inhabiting a powerful part, they may wish to put the cloth over a chair or a pile of cushions to show how 'big' the part is. If it's a part that stands up for the client, they may wish to lay down a sword alongside the cloth. Or if it's a young childlike part of them, they may wish to choose a cuddly toy to bring that part to life.

Once the client has the part represented in the way that is right for them, they step off the carpet and come back to their chair. The client can now view that part of themselves from the outside. This allows time for reflection and discussion as the client sees the part from this new perspective. The practitioner will often have written down some of the words the client said whilst they were in the part. The client then has the opportunity to look at the representation of that part, hear the practitioner read out the words, and experience that part of themselves from a stepped-back place.

Once our client Joe is back in his seat, he watches the pale blue part and hears Sam read out the words that were spoken. As the practitioner, Sam had felt very tenderly towards the little boy when he was speaking to him on the carpet. However, Joe's reaction on hearing the words read back is one of revulsion: 'How pathetic, I just feel so ashamed of that part. I want to give him a good kicking. He has no backbone. He's an embarrassment. He's just got victim written all over him. I don't even want to look at him.'

From his training Sam immediately recognises this as another significant part of Joe speaking up. A part that is ashamed of this blue part of himself. He asks Joe if he'd like to explore this part next, or if there is a different direction he'd like to take, and in this way their work together continues.

So, in Healing The Shadow we go through a process of representing parts of the client on a carpet in the middle of the room. However, we need to bring more structure and focus than simply exploring many parts of the client. We want the session to have direction, and we want the client to be in charge of their session. With such deep work we need to be sure that the client is in control and is consciously guiding the session at all times – both for their emotional safety and so that they can get the outcome they are looking for.

With this in mind, at the start of each session, well before getting into any parts work, we ask the client what they want to have happen for themselves during that session. We spend time talking to them about the shift they wish to see inside them, and we get all the background information we need so we can attune to the client and understand what they are wanting from the session.

We call their desired outcome the Guiding Want. Once we have established this clearly, we then move ahead and start exploring the parts of them that they see as relevant to this. We all have so many different parts that without the focus of the Guiding Want to keep us on track we could spend days exploring many wild and wonderful parts of ourselves without ever getting any closer to the outcome we desire.

With the Guiding Want directing us, we aim to build up a picture on the carpet of all the relevant parts of the client. In this way the patterns that live in the client's inner world begin to reveal themselves to us. Joe's Guiding Want was to feel more confidence and to have a greater sense of power and agency in the world, so Sam is helping Joe to represent all the parts of him that are related to this.

However, the shadow is hard to pin down, and we know that aspects of ourselves that we find hard to accept can be disowned as parts of ourselves and projected onto others around us. This psychological process is a core principle of shadow work and is known as projection.

So we don't restrict our exploration simply to parts living in the client – we also explore any people, organisations, animals, groups or places that are having an impact on the client's life. This ensures we explore the whole of the client's world – not just the parts they are comfortable with or easily aware of.

As well as projecting unowned aspects of ourselves onto others, we can also project the qualities of key people from our past onto others. These qualities may be positive aspects of a loving person or destructive qualities of a cruel parent or teacher or adult from our early lives. When we project these qualities onto another person, we then begin to interact with this person in the same way as we interacted with the person from our past. This psychological process is closely related to projection and is known as transference.

Transference is a very powerful process, and it is essential that an understanding of this is included when we are working with the shadow. With our understanding of projection and transference, we can see that it is important to include external influences in our work if we wish to have the whole of the client's inner world accurately represented. This is why we make sure to give the opportunity for other people, groups and so on to be represented on the carpet as well as parts of the client themselves.

Let's go back to Joe in his session. Sam has just suggested that Joe could step into the part of himself that is embarrassed of the blue part. However, it turns out Joe isn't really interested in exploring that part. After some discussion he decides he wants to represent his boss on the carpet, the one who is destroying his confidence and causing him high levels of fear.

In response to this Sam gets out a whiteboard and asks Joe to place it on the carpet to represent his boss. He then invites Joe to choose a coloured cloth to go with the whiteboard. Joe chooses a dark grey cloth and places it over the board like a cloak, leaving space for Sam to write on the white surface.

Sam now asks Joe to tell him what messages he hears from his boss at work. These are not necessarily words his boss actually says, but the messages Joe picks up from him from the way he behaves.

Joe is quickly able to list the messages he receives:

You are pathetic.

You have no backbone.

I just want to kick you out of here.

You are revolting.

You are an embarrassment to the company.

Sam then writes these messages up on the whiteboard.

You may notice that whilst Joe didn't show any interest in representing and exploring the part of himself that shames the blue part, he has, nevertheless, ended up bringing a similar part onto the carpet in the form of his boss. The messages Joe receives from his boss are almost word for word the same as the comments he made about the blue part of himself earlier in the session. In Joe's boss we seem to have found another part that is ashamed of the blue part. So despite Joe choosing not to step into the part in himself that feels this, a similar part has still shown up on his carpet.

We find that the work unfolds in this way. With the practitioner following what the client wants, the parts that are relevant for the client's healing and growth will appear on the carpet one way or another. As practitioners we can trust this, and we can allow things to unfold, rather than having any kind of agenda as to what we think will work best for the client. Conversely, if the client is not ready to explore a particular part of themselves, then no amount of encouragement or suggestion from the practitioner will persuade them to go there; furthermore, such encouragement can cause disharmony in the relationship between client and practitioner. We find that if we follow the client, this work unfolds in the way that is right for them, and they have insight and understanding at the time that is right for them and their journey.

So although Sam spotted Joe's strong negative reaction to the blue part and suggested this might be another part of Joe they could explore together, he didn't question it when Joe chose not to step into that part. He simply moved on to the part that Joe *was* interested in, which was his boss. He trusted this was the right part to work with next in this session. It seems for now it is more appropriate for Joe to see these qualities in his boss, where he can hate them, rather than inside himself, where he would have to own them as a part of him.

Joe and Sam continue to explore different parts. First Joe steps into a part that is angry with his boss. He then steps into a part that feels ashamed of not being able to stand up for himself.

Then Joe and Sam take a break and review the scene on the carpet together. When looking at the carpet, Joe recognises that the messages from his boss are similar to the messages he got from his stepdad, who used to beat him as a child. Joe tells Sam how his stepdad would run around the house looking for him, and how he hid under the stairs hoping he wouldn't be found.

From Sam's understanding as a practitioner, it now looks possible that Joe may have transferred his stepdad onto his boss. This doesn't mean that his boss doesn't have some, or all, of the qualities Joe is seeing in him – it just means that Joe is particularly disturbed by these qualities in a way that other people might not be. From the disgust Joe showed when he looked at the blue part of himself, it also looks possible that Joe has developed an Inner Stepdad part, which talks to him internally in a similar way to the way his stepdad used to talk to him. This isn't work for today, but Sam will hold an awareness of these parts and their origins, and he will be prepared if they come up again in future sessions as the work progresses.

With Joe's insight that the messages he is receiving from his boss are the same as the ones he received from his stepdad, we now have two scenes on the carpet in our mind's eye: Joe as an adult feeling low in confidence, with his boss giving him destructive messages, and also Joe aged three, scared of his stepdad and hiding from him under the stairs, with his stepdad looking for him and calling him names. Sam asks Joe how he is viewing the scene – is it a present-day scene or does he see it as a childhood scene?

Joe is now entranced by the scene of himself as a three-year-old hiding from his stepdad. He tells Sam this is what he is seeing on the carpet in front of him. The current-day situation has served to highlight the childhood memory, but it no longer feels relevant. So together this is how they now view the scene on the carpet. It's as if this scene from Joe's childhood is still alive inside him and having an impact on his adult life.

Since Joe's Guiding Want for the session was to feel more confident and to have a sense of power and agency in his life, Sam now focuses on this. He asks Joe what needs to change in the scene he sees before him in order for him to feel more confidence and to have the sense of power and agency he is looking for. Joe reflects for a while and then he says the little boy needs some support and care, and also someone needs to stand up to his stepdad and tell him to leave little Joe alone.

Joe now has the opportunity to bring some healing to the point of origin of this emotional wound. The process work he does will change the pattern he is carrying in his inner world around his abuse. This change will then filter up from his unconscious and effect a change in the dynamic he is experiencing with his boss, as well as in other places in his life where he is experiencing a lack of confidence.

From this glimpse into Joe's session, we can see that parts work is almost infinitely flexible and unfolds in the way that is right for the client on that day. In this session Joe's work has taken him back to a painful childhood memory that has emerged and is calling for healing. On other days his work might feel and look very different to this.

A few weeks earlier Joe had a session where he worked on difficulties making a decision about moving house. He spoke to two different parts of himself – one that wanted to move to the countryside and one that wanted to stay in the city. Sam then facilitated a conversation between these two parts so that they could hear each other's point of view and reach a new way of looking at the decision that lay ahead. Getting these two opposing parts speaking to each other brought an end to months of fear and indecision and opened the door for Joe to move forward with his plans.

Neither client nor practitioner can know how the work is going to unfold on any given day until they start exploring together, and working with what arises in response to the client's Guiding Want.

2.

Process Work

In Healing The Shadow we work with the idea that we all carry certain patterns, or 'dynamics', within our inner world. These patterns were often set very early in our lives when difficult things happened to us that we couldn't process effectively.

We find that when people don't process a traumatic event or situation, the dynamics of that situation become imprinted on their psyche. As they continue with their lives, they find their outer world reflects this imprint that they carry within them. This means that, paradoxically, even when people leave the original distressing situation behind, they tend to experience similar scenarios playing out in their lives in different ways, despite the fact that they are now well away from the situation that caused the imprint.

This chapter demonstrates the method we use in Healing The Shadow to rewrite these imprints so they can better serve us in our current lives.

Let's go back to our client Joe. At age three his father left, and his mum's new partner moved in. Joe was very sad, confused and upset. On top of this, his new stepdad took against him and shouted at him and put him down. Sometimes he was physically violent. Joe was terrified, and his mum wasn't able to support him or protect him. She wasn't able to stand up to her new partner – partly because she herself was scared of him and partly because she and her son were financially dependent on him.

As an adult now, having left his home situation well behind, and even having moved countries, Joe continually finds himself in situations with men who are emotionally abusive to him, where he feels small and scared. Mostly this occurs with authority figures of some kind – with managers and bosses in a variety of different work situations.

As a young boy, the dynamic of an abusive man terrorising a small, frightened child was imprinted into Joe's inner world. Ever since then he has carried this dynamic around inside him, and his outer world has evolved to reflect this. He constantly finds himself part of these kinds of situations, where he is experiencing abuse and intimidation and is feeling small and frightened.

These experiences are set in motion by real events, and the fact that Joe carries this dynamic inside him does not, of course, excuse the behaviour of men who have been disrespectful to him in his adult life. However, having an understanding that he carries this dynamic inside himself does give Joe more awareness and choice as to how he behaves within those situations, and it points a way forward for his healing.

Up until now Joe has had very little conscious control over these situations and how he experiences them. The emotions have been consciously experienced but the mechanism behind his reactions works on an unconscious level that is beyond his control.

As a child Joe had only two choices: hide or experience verbal or physical abuse. He had no support, he had no physical strength, he had no money or resources, which would have allowed him to leave the situation, so his options, as for all children, were very limited. As an adult he now has other choices available when confronted by men he finds abusive. He could stand up for himself and look for support. He could leave the situation or follow a complaints procedure. He has many more options available to him than he did as a child. However, rather than choosing these options, Joe tends to respond with the well-known childhood responses because these fit with the way his inner world looks, and they replay and reinforce the dynamic he carries inside.

So healing needs to take place in the dynamic Joe is carrying inside him before he is able to release himself from this pattern and explore these new ways of being. Since the outer world reflects the inner world, Joe needs to change the scene he carries inside him if he is to change the experiences he is having in his life. If he can successfully bring new adults into the scene who are caring and protective towards him, then he can change the picture on the carpet from one of aggression and fear to one of love and safety. This can then change the dynamic that is imprinted within him. This is not easy work; however, once this change has taken place and been integrated, his outer world will, as always, evolve to reflect his inner world, and a new scene of love and safety will start to play out in Joe's life rather than the old scene of neglect and abuse.

This is the basis of the process work we do in Healing The Shadow. We work with the scene on the carpet to bring healing to the emotional wounds the client is carrying. At the same time as bringing healing to the client, this work *also* changes the way their inner world looks and feels, and it changes the imprint they are carrying inside them. Before this healing work takes place, the old imprint plays out constantly in their life, but once the new imprint is in place this will now start playing out instead, and many aspects of the client's life will change because of that. It is hugely empowering to know that we can bring about such significant change in our lives by doing this inner work and updating the dynamics we carry inside.

So once we have the dynamic laid out on the carpet, with all the relevant parts represented, the practitioner then asks the client what needs to change in the scene so that they can have the shift they wish to see inside themselves. The client will always know what needs to happen, and following the client will give a much deeper and more integrated change than if the practitioner were to impose their own ideas.

At the end of the last chapter Joe told Sam he wanted the little boy to have some support, and he wanted someone there in the scene to stand up to his stepdad. Let's continue from there.

When asked which needs to happen first, Joe says someone needs to stand up to the stepdad and get him to leave, because the little boy couldn't possibly receive any care or support when the stepdad was raging around the house and terrifying him. Sam and Joe then talk for a while about who that person could be who could come in and stand up to his stepdad. Joe thinks a firefighter would be a good strong person who knows about right and wrong and would be able to come into the house and tell his stepdad he has to go.

So Sam invites Joe to choose a coloured cloth to step into so he can inhabit this firefighter's energy. He chooses a red cloth and wraps it around his shoulders and takes on the qualities of the firefighter – strong, knowing right from wrong, protective, confident. Sam offers Joe the opportunity to use a bat and a cushion to express the anger he feels towards the stepdad, and to use that energy to drive the stepdad out of the room. Joe readily agrees. He has a lot of unexpressed anger towards his stepdad. This is the perfect time to harness that anger and to both express it *and* use it for good. He can use it to remove his stepdad from the scene on the carpet and protect his three-year-old self.

Anger gets stuck in us when it can't be used in a purposeful way. Joe's anger was stuck in him as a child because he couldn't use it to stand up to his stepdad. If he tried, his mum got upset and his stepdad got even angrier. He quickly discovered it was pointless and just led to more pain. Here he can use his anger to finally put things right.

This, of course, doesn't change what happened to Joe as a child. However, it does change the dynamic that is imprinted inside him. It changes the way he holds the memory. It brings a new, strong figure into the scene. This is now a resource that Joe will have inside him when he faces new situations of abusive behaviour.

In adult life Joe's anger has tended to come out as impotent rage, which has not served him and has left him alienated and afraid of this side of himself. Doing this work can give Joe the experience of his anger being used for good. He can get to know it as a powerful resource that can serve him in his life.

Of course, such a full expression of physical anger is not likely to be appropriate or necessary in the workplace. However, we find that people only need to go through some kind of an anger gateway like this once in order to get in touch with their good, effective anger. They need to have this full expression of their anger and power so that they can feel it and know that it lives inside them. We provide a space where this can happen in a safe, shame-free way, where no one gets hurt and the outcome is a positive one for the client. This new connection to their anger can then serve them by giving strength and determination to their words and behaviour so that people take them seriously and respect them. Others will now be able to sense the power and confidence behind their words.

So Joe steps into the role of the firefighter and, with careful instructions from Sam, he stands up to his stepdad and tells him to get out and get away from little Joe. He says many of the things he was unable to say to his stepdad when he was a child about how wrong his behaviour was. He uses the bat and the cushion to help him express his anger and to give him a real sense of his own power. He builds up his energy until he feels stronger than his stepdad and then, using the full force of his voice and beating the cushion with all his strength, he tells him to go. As Joe bellows out his command, Sam moves the stepdad slowly off the carpet and out of Joe's world.

Sam celebrates this achievement with Joe and invites him to see how different his inner world looks now. The stepdad is off the carpet and a strong firefighter is keeping him away.

Some people choose to come back into the scene as their adult selves to carry out this kind of work rather than using an imaginary figure as Joe has done. As far as Joe's healing process is concerned, it doesn't matter which route he has taken – what matters is that it is Joe himself who has stepped in to do this, whether he is representing a firefighter or himself. It is a part of Joe that has stood up to his stepdad, even though he used the image of a firefighter to help him to find this energy within him. So ultimately the energetic shift has happened inside Joe himself, and he has grown a new part which has the ability to stand up for him.

The scene inside Joe is different now that he has this strong, protective firefighter figure on his side. As the work integrates within him, this new scene will start to play out in his outer world and he will start to stand up for himself and protect himself when he is being treated badly. This will increase his sense of power and agency in his life, which is one of the things he told Sam he wanted at the start of the session.

Next, if you remember, Joe wanted some support for the little boy. Again, Sam asks him how he would like to do this.

Who could come and support the little boy and give him the care he needs? Joe chooses a neighbour who was always very kind to him and used to babysit for him sometimes. Her name was Ava. Again, Sam asks Joe to choose a coloured cloth for Ava. He chooses a beautiful golden cloth and as he puts on this cloth he takes on the qualities of Ava – kind, understanding, gentle, caring, warm and soft. He then goes to be with the little boy and give him some comfort and support. This is tender work as, in the role of Ava, he brings love, understanding and compassion to his younger self. He holds the little boy in his arms and rocks and soothes him and tells him he's safe. After about twenty minutes this work is complete, and he comes back to his seat to discuss it with Sam. Joe is deeply touched by what has happened and has tears in his eyes as he feels this compassion for his younger self. Once they have talked for a while, Sam offers him the opportunity to step back into the blue part, into the three-year-old boy, so that he can receive this support from Ava and see what it feels like.

Joe puts the blue cloth on and settles down again into the thoughts and feelings of the little three-year-old boy who lives inside him. He wraps Ava's beautiful golden cloth around himself, and Sam reads out the words that Ava spoke. Joe feels deeply peaceful. Sam puts on some music and reads the words out again. Joe soaks up this new support and care and understanding, allowing it to flow into his body, and letting the new feeling of comfort and safety slowly ease away his fear and distress. He talks back to Ava and tells her about how frightened he has been and how glad he is that she is there.

Joe now has another new resource in his inner world: a part that is loving, caring and understanding towards him, and can support him when he is upset about how other people are treating him. He has grown a new part that is on his side, and with this his confidence and sense of self will grow.

So after all this work the scene inside Joe now looks very different. He has a strong, protective firefighter keeping his stepdad away, and he has a loving, supportive woman holding him and caring for him. Carrying this new scene inside him, Joe is now much more likely to be able to stand up for himself and support himself in difficult situations. However, there is something more magical than this at play. This new scene is also likely to result in *other* people accepting and supporting Joe, and in *other* people standing up for him. So in doing this work he has opened a gateway to accepting and receiving support and protection in his life, as well as to providing it for himself.

We find this kind of process work extremely effective. It is far more powerful than simply talking about the changes someone would like to make in the scene, or rearranging the parts on the carpet to create the scene they want. Process work invites the client to consciously and deliberately step into parts on the carpet and to do embodied work which brings about a change in the way the scene on the carpet *lives inside them.* This kind of process work actually changes something inside the client's body and being, rather than just in their intellectual understanding. Consequently, the new scene now lives *inside* the client, not just in the representations on the carpet.

Joe's experience in this session gives a brief glimpse into the process work used in Healing The Shadow. To allow time for this process work to be carried out safely and effectively we tend to work in longer sessions, usually between two and five hours in length. We find that every process looks very, very different, since each session is directed entirely by the client. We offer a wide range of processes that enable us to follow the client as closely as possible. With our support the client can create the process that is exactly right for them on that day.

Another reason we like to use process work in Healing The Shadow is because it allows the practitioner to be fully present in the first part of the session without needing to strive for change. Knowing that a phase of change is coming later, the practitioner can accept and welcome all that arises as the client explores all the different parts of themselves. This allows a unique form of listening and presence to occur whilst the client is exploring.

Shadow work is complex, and for many of us it is a lifetime's journey. Joe's work with this scene doesn't end with the work he has done here today. The dynamics that live inside us can play out in many ways. As we have seen in this session, Joe's pattern plays out with him feeling scared and low in confidence at work, where he has an abusive boss. We have also seen that it plays out inside Joe himself, where Joe is critical and intolerant of the blue frightened part that lives inside him.

What hasn't been explored in this session, however, is the way this pattern plays out between Joe and his sons, where Joe is now the intolerant one and his sons are small and scared of him at times. Joe hasn't talked to Sam yet about the difficulty he is having parenting his sons, as he feels too much shame about this side of his life.

In the months following the session, Joe finds his work situation much improved, and he feels more powerful and more confident. He starts to stand up for himself, and his boss starts to treat him with more respect, and even offers him a pay rise. However, in his home life Joe is still struggling with his behaviour towards his sons. He is unable to control the critical part of him which slips out and wounds them.

Picture the new scene Joe has created in his inner world. There is a strong, protective firefighter part keeping the abusive stepdad out and there is a loving Ava part supporting the frightened part of Joe. However, the stepdad energy is not gone – it is still there, just off the carpet, threatening to come back if the firefighter drops their guard.

This is because, as we have seen, this stepdad energy lives inside Joe now: it is a part of him. We can never truly get rid of parts of ourselves – we can only get to know them and transform them. So although Joe has learnt to stand up to people he finds abusive in the outer world, he is still left with an inner part that behaves in an abusive way, both towards himself and towards others.

Ultimately, hard though it will be, Joe will need to accept that a part of his stepdad now lives inside him. This is the only way he can completely release the hold this dynamic has on him. He will need to get to know that side of himself, understand it and learn to control it. Through this process, he will also be able to discover the gifts that part could bring.

For example, the power inside this abusive side of Joe, once harnessed and separated out from the abusive behaviour, could then be used to serve Joe in his life. It could help him to stand up for himself, and it could help him to step up and take on roles of authority where he could use his power to serve others. This way the dynamic would be fully transformed inside him. There would no longer be a bad, scary figure there – this figure would have been transformed into a powerful ally in Joe's life.

The work of owning dark and destructive parts of ourselves is very challenging to undertake, as it involves us stepping into and becoming a side of ourselves we are scared of and never want to be like. We are stepping into a part of ourselves we normally spend all our time trying *not* to inhabit. However, in a safe, well-held space we can, if we wish, take the risk of stepping into this side of ourselves, knowing that there will be no real-world consequences from doing this in a therapeutic space, and knowing that we are being supported by a practitioner who has travelled this path before us.

As we release the energy that's held in this part, it can begin to transform. Parts of us can only be 'bad' when they are kept in shadow. Once we get to know them, we can learn to have control over them. We can then choose whether or not to act from this side of ourselves. Further to this, once such a part has been released and allowed to express itself, we find that it gets in touch with its true purpose. We can then ask it what it really wants to do with all this energy. We find there is gold buried in our shadows, and when these parts originated, long ago, they were in some way trying to help us. So we can find the gifts this part has to offer us, and we can separate these out from the destructive behaviours. We can then choose to use the power this part holds in a way that serves us and others in our lives.

We call dark and destructive parts of ourselves Persecutor parts, and working with Persecutor parts is some of the most transformational work we do in Healing The Shadow. Once these parts of us are owned and transformed, a deep peace reigns inside. We have ended the internal battle, and can come home to ourselves, knowing, accepting and loving ourselves in a new way.

If Joe undertook this work, the scene on his carpet would then be very different. There would be no 'bad' stepdad in the picture – the stepdad energy would have changed into a powerful figure who was a positive resource for Joe. As this work integrated within Joe, he would no longer behave in an attacking way towards his children, nor would he behave in an attacking way towards the small, vulnerable part of himself.

This internal battle is often the one that causes us most pain, when parts inside us are turned against each other. Though not externally obvious to others, this can be the cause of depression, self-harm, addiction and other hidden damaging patterns.

When the time is right Joe will bring the issue of his relationship with his sons to a session with Sam and he will have the opportunity to do this work if he wishes. In the meantime, he has plenty to do integrating his new, protective part and practising standing up for himself and defending himself, and also caring for and supporting himself when he feels vulnerable. It is important to have these new resources well established before he sets himself up for further, more challenging, work.

3.

The Shadow

Our shadows make themselves known to us in the sides of ourselves we struggle to understand or accept – aspects we fear may emotionally overwhelm us or cause harm to ourselves or others. We all have sides that cause shame and confusion, and they can be the source of much pain and difficulty. Paradoxically, the more we try to ignore or hide these sides of ourselves, the greater their capacity to disrupt our lives – they can cause relationship rupture, hold us back from going for our goals, sap our energy and stop us from expressing all of who we are.

An example of a shadow

Our client Joe has two sons, David and Isaac. Since David turned three Joe has had a hard time with parenting them. As mentioned earlier, despite his intention to be a loving parent, he often feels shaming and critical towards his boys. He has lashed out at them emotionally and, on occasions, physically. He feels a huge amount of shame about this, and hasn't yet been able to bring himself to talk about it with his practitioner, Sam.

What Joe is experiencing in his relationship with his sons is the effect of a shadow part of himself. This shadow part is driving his behaviour from behind the scenes. It is out of his conscious control, and it has the power to override his loving intentions and to cause harm in his relationship with his boys.

Joe loves his sons. He invests a huge amount of time and energy in helping them with their homework and taking them out to play sports. He only ever wants the best for them. Yet this shaming and critical behaviour seems to come from nowhere and causes immense damage.

It mostly happens with his oldest son, David. Joe is calm one minute and the next minute his face is tight and tense and he is unable to disguise his disdain for his son. The criticism comes pouring out. He doesn't see this behaviour as belonging to him. It's not the way he wants to behave. It comes out of nowhere and goes again just as quickly. He feels so ashamed of this behaviour that he can't ever fully admit to himself that he acts in such hateful ways.

This example is typical of the way a shadow part can wreak havoc in our lives. To understand this better, let's take a further look at shadow parts and how they form.

The formation of our shadows

As discussed previously, in Healing The Shadow we work with the idea that we are all made up of many different parts. Some of these parts we are aware of and happy with, others we know well but are *not* happy with. We'd rather they weren't there, or we'd like them to change.

In addition to this there are yet other parts of ourselves of which we are largely in denial, and of which we have little clear awareness. They flit around just out of sight, coming suddenly and going again just as quickly. They live in a dreamlike place. We don't talk about these parts of ourselves to anyone; we don't even think about them when we are on our own. They are largely missing from our conscious knowledge of who we are and, as a result of this, they are not under our conscious control. They take us by surprise, we don't recognise them as aspects of ourselves, and we can suffer much pain and confusion as these hidden parts run things from the shadows.

Let's look a little more deeply at Joe's situation and how he came to find himself behaving in the way he does with his sons.

For Joe as a child, behaving like his stepdad was the worst thing he could possibly imagine. He made a promise to himself when he was still a young boy that as a grown-up he would *never* behave in the way his stepdad was behaving towards him. His mother often talked to him about what a bad person his stepdad was. She would cry and tell Joe he was her little prince and she was so happy that Joe was so different from his stepdad. Once Joe left school, he trained as a social worker in order to bring kindness to children and to do everything he could to ensure children didn't have to suffer at the hands of abusive adults.

Yet later in life Joe found he had a part of himself that was *exactly* like his stepdad.

We all have cruel and judgemental sides of us, but when Joe found himself feeling this way he pushed it so far out of his consciousness that he never learnt to get to know this side of himself. Instead, he denied that he was like that. He distanced himself from this part of him. Most of the time he found he could control it. The thoughts played out in his head constantly, he couldn't prevent that, but they were rarely spoken out loud to others. On the few occasions these judgemental thoughts *did* slip out, he later minimised or dismissed what he had said. He simply couldn't admit to himself that he had this behaviour in him.

Joe was not consciously denying this part – it was simply a reflex action, happening as a result of a decision made long ago.

Paradoxically, because Joe kept this part of him so buried and hidden away, it began to cause him more and more trouble. Once his sons came along, it was harder for him to deny this side of himself. He was confused by his behaviour and ashamed of it. He was devastated to think that he may be harming his sons by the way he spoke to them.

All of us have shadow sides and, in a similar way to Joe, most people find that the root goes back to childhood. Shadows are formed when we cut off, repress or deny any part of ourselves, and we *all* do this in childhood – it is an essential part of surviving and adapting to the world in which we find ourselves.

For example, if our father tells us it is wrong to get angry, then we may take our anger and hide it away in order to gain his approval and love. We may try to convince ourselves that we don't have anger, it is not a part of us. This decision will help us to survive our childhood in the best way possible. Or if our mother can't bear our tears, and turns away from us and ignores us when we cry, we will learn to hide our sadness and not to turn to her for support and care. Or if our playfulness causes our mother to spin into a rage, then we will quickly learn to hide this joyful part of ourselves so that we don't evoke her wrath.

So we put parts of ourselves into shadow as we react with entirely appropriate, sometimes life-saving, responses to the situations in which we find ourselves. These are the absolute best decisions we could make at the time, and they allow us to survive, and even enjoy, what might otherwise have been intolerable. Our shadow contains all the parts of us we silence and hide: characteristics that might have been counterproductive or unsafe for us to express, or characteristics we found so unbearable in others that we couldn't face accepting them within ourselves.

If we continue with the example where a child has put their anger into shadow, it's important to understand that it is not the anger itself that is the problem here. Anger is an entirely natural and necessary part of us. Anger helps to let us know when we are being treated badly or when our boundaries are being crossed. It gives us the energy to take action in the world and to stand up for ourselves and protect those we love. If we have our anger in shadow, it is not anger that is the problem – it is actually *losing touch* with our anger that is the problem. It is the fact that we don't know and can't healthily express this side of ourselves, and it is the behaviours we employ to try to keep our anger hidden that cast a shadow in our lives.

Another example might be someone who has put their sensuality into shadow. If a child has been told it is shameful to enjoy soft blankets and clothes, and to like feeling their body and being touched and held, then they will try to deny this side of themselves. They will lose connection with their love of their body and their enjoyment of sensual experiences. As they become an adult, they may find it difficult to connect with themselves and others because they are trying to keep their sensuality hidden. They may become cold and distant, unable to ask for the touch and connection they want and feeling a lot of shame around their bodily desires. As denying this becomes harder and harder to sustain, their need could overwhelm them and burst out in uncontrolled ways, such as having affairs, the compulsive use of sex workers or getting drunk and seeking sexual connection in unsafe ways. This shadow could also show up in cruel and shaming behaviours towards people who *are* able to be openly sensual and are in touch with their body's needs and desires.

Shadows take many different forms. We may have hidden our jealousy, our anger, our selfishness, our fear, our leadership ability, our desire for connection, our chattiness, our playfulness, our sexuality, our deep knowing, our love for people we're not meant to love... the list is endless, and different for each of us, depending on the culture and the particular family environment in which we grew up.

Some of us had sudden shocking moments when we knew we needed to put a side of ourselves away. For example, if both our parents died when we were young, we may have realised there was no longer any place for our childlike nature, and so we put that side of ourselves away. Or if we lashed out one day in anger, hitting our younger brother, we may have been shamed and punished for this and decided our anger had to be hidden away if we were ever to be accepted by our parents.

Others of us received a slow drip, drip of 'hints' that told us parts of us were not acceptable. For example, we may have heard things like: 'Be brave.' 'Boys don't cry.' 'Nice girls don't do that.' 'Be Mummy's good boy.' 'Don't be a sissy.' 'You wouldn't want to disappoint your dad.' 'You don't look very pretty when you do that.' These kinds of comments send children powerful messages about which parts of them will and will not be tolerated by those around them.

Or maybe it was looks or actions that made us realise it wasn't safe to express certain aspects of ourselves. Maybe we saw others getting punished for expressing these sides of themselves, so we learnt to keep those parts of us well hidden. We all have nuanced and individual experiences of how we learnt to deny or hide parts of ourselves, and by the time we are adults we all have many different parts in shadow.

For example, our client Joe hasn't only hidden away his shaming and critical part – he has also put his vulnerability into shadow. It wasn't safe for him to show this as a child. His stepdad beat him and tormented him if he showed weakness, and his mother needed him to be strong for her, as she wasn't emotionally capable of holding his upset and tears. So he hid his vulnerability away and went through life being cheerful and helpful and never sharing his sadness and fear with others. He wasn't even aware he carried sadness and fear until he started doing shadow work with Sam. We don't only hide our shadow sides from others – we can hide them away so well that even we ourselves are unaware that we have these qualities. This was the case for Joe, and when he started exploring his inner world he was shocked to find so much sadness and fear inside himself.

Hiding parts of ourselves away like this is an essential process to go through as we grow up. However, as we reach adulthood, we can find that trying to keep these sides of ourselves hidden is causing us more problems than it solves. The original reason for hiding these parts has receded. The way we are behaving makes less and less sense. We may still want the approval of our family and community, but we no longer depend on it for our survival.

Yet the parts we hid away in childhood remain in the shadows, where they can cause havoc and disrupt our lives. We explode with rage when we least want to – our shadow anger has overwhelmed us. We are irresponsible at times when we need to step up – our shadow playfulness has overwhelmed us. We are highly dependent and demanding in our relationships – our shadow need for love has overwhelmed us.

So our shadows are parts of ourselves we experience as overwhelming or controlling; things we find ourselves doing even though we swore we never would; parts of ourselves we try to hide from others but that burst out unexpectedly; sides of ourselves we don't feel able to own; certain aspects of ourselves we cannot accept; certain behaviours for which we are unable to forgive ourselves; certain personality traits we deny we have.

Looking at our shadows is tender and vulnerable territory. Acknowledging and exploring these hidden sides of ourselves can shake us to the core. These hidden, unexplored parts require a safe and accepting space and skilled and sensitive holding if they are to come out of the shadows and make themselves known. It is then possible for us to accept and get to know these sides of ourselves and learn to control their destructive impulses.

Finding gold in our shadows

Gaining control over these destructive sides of ourselves is only a part of the story. In Healing The Shadow we don't work simply to rid our clients' lives of difficulties or to 'tame' their shadow sides. We hold the space for so much more than this. We take the energy in these powerful sides of ourselves and we find the gold and gifts that they hold. We transform the 'negative', 'destructive' parts of our psyche into powerful resources and allies. We free up the gifts that have been locked away in these sides of ourselves and we reclaim these hidden qualities and use them to create lives we never previously thought were possible.

We not only learn to control the behaviours that aren't serving us, but we also find that within this same part of us are the power and wisdom needed to live the life we have always wanted to live. This is what makes shadow work so powerful. It's not just about healing – it's about transformation. It's about taking the worst and most shameful aspects of ourselves and turning them into our greatest assets, turning them into gold.

Let's look at the process behind this transformation in a little more detail. Whatever aspects of ourselves we have hidden away, however unacceptable or destructive we may believe them to be, we find that there is always a kernel of essential 'life force' we have hidden away too, along with all the 'bad' stuff we were trying to avoid. In hiding this side away, we have prevented ourselves from accessing this essential life force and we find ourselves hampered in life. We don't have access to the whole of ourselves. For example, we may find that we can't enjoy our free time as we don't know how to relax and play, or that we can't stand up for ourselves because we don't have access to our anger, or maybe we find that we can't love freely because we learnt there were too many risks to this… We now find that we need the very parts of ourselves we have hidden away.

To be clear, we don't believe there are any 'negative' aspects to our psyche. All parts of us are necessary and have an important role to play. A part of us only begins to take on negative qualities when we decide it is unacceptable for some reason and we put it into shadow. We then lose contact with this essential life gift. It becomes unintegrated in our lives and operates beyond our conscious control in ways that don't serve us.

So, for example, we may have seen anger being used dangerously or abusively when we were a child, and we made a very wise decision to hide our anger away so that we would never act like that. We never want to be a dangerous or abusive person, as we've seen how much harm it can do. However, once we get to adulthood, we find that in locking away our anger we have also locked away our ability to stand up for ourselves, to set our boundaries, to protect ourselves and what is precious to us and to go for what we want in life – these are some of the many positive aspects that healthy anger has to offer.

So it is with any other aspect of ourselves we've hidden – each has a golden side we could really do with if we want to live a rich and full life. We can see, with the above example of anger, that reclaiming healthy anger would mean we'd be able to set our boundaries more clearly and respectfully, stand up for ourselves with strength and dignity, and forge forward in creating the life we want. This would lead to healthier relationships with others and greater fulfilment, and ultimately we would feel better about the kind of person we are and be more comfortable in ourselves. So as we gain conscious control over our anger, we can discover the hidden value it holds and we can use it to serve us in our lives.

Alternatively, when growing up we may have been told we needed to be tough to get on in life and that we had to force our way forward to get ahead. We were taunted as being weak if we showed kindness, so we hid that side of ourselves away. We believed kindness was dangerous and debilitating and that we were weak and shameful for having this in us. We came to completely deny that side of ourselves and this enabled us to gain our parents' respect and approval. However, in adult life, although we find ourselves successful, we are lonely. The kindness we were taught to despise is now a quality we desperately need in order to find friendship and connection and a sense of community.

Unfortunately though, when we try to show kindness to people they find us 'fake' or 'needy'. They take advantage of us and we become an object of ridicule. This is because we don't know that part of ourselves and we feel shame about it, so it comes out in shadowy ways that others find uncomfortable. We can't trust ourselves to show kindness now, even when we want to, as it only seems to lead to more pain rather than to connection.

What is necessary here is for us to take the time to get to know this kindness that we learnt was so weak and debilitating. We need to take away the shame we feel about this part of our nature. We need to understand this part of ourselves and find protection and guidance for it so it only shows up when it is appropriate and doesn't cause us further pain. We can then integrate this loving side of ourselves back into our lives and allow it to flow naturally in a way that can bring true connection and friendship into our lives.

The same is true for any part we hold in shadow. As we get to know it and take control over it, we discover and release the life-changing gifts it has to offer, which have been locked away from us for most of our lives.

In order for this to happen, we, as Healing The Shadow practitioners, believe that such parts need to be fully explored and witnessed. Talking about our shadow parts may give us an intellectual insight and understanding, but it does not give us an embodied and integrated experience of those parts living inside us. There is so much energy tied up with these parts. Talking about our cruel side is very different from stepping in and inhabiting that cruel part of ourselves and allowing the cruel energy to speak and act. Talking about the sad part of us is very different from inhabiting our sadness and experiencing the full depths of the grief that lives there, and the sounds and bodily movements that come with this. By us inhabiting these parts fully, the energy they hold is able to move and shift. We believe this full embodiment of our shadow parts is what is required if those parts of us are to be truly brought out of shadow and transformed.

A huge amount of power and energy is tied up in our shadow parts. They are vital parts of us, wanting expression and striving to be seen and heard, yet we are spending a huge amount of our time and energy trying to hold them down and keep them hidden. This can really sap our life force. When we bring these parts out of shadow, we free up all the energy that's been locked away – the energy of the part itself *and* the energy we've been using to try and keep it hidden. This power is now available to us to use in our lives in any way we wish. We feel more alive and vibrant and can engage in life more fully.

Working with risks

Whilst there are life-changing benefits to working with the shadow, there are also risks. There is a huge amount of fear associated with our shadows. We put parts into shadow when we are in frightening situations as a child and our survival depends on it. To reclaim the shadow means going back into those frightening moments, as we saw with Joe in his piece of work, and it means feeling the painful feelings associated with them. We have powerful parts of us trying to protect us from re-experiencing those feelings – with good reason. Such strong feelings can overwhelm us if we are not resourced to hold them.

We all have our own natural pathway to healing and growth. Much of the work we do in Healing The Shadow is working with the parts that resist change and growth. We welcome and value these parts just as much as any others, and spend much time getting to know and understand them. We don't work to change these parts, as we know they are there for good reason and have the best interests of the client at heart. We simply welcome them and get to know them, honouring them for the tremendously important role they have played.

We know that if and when the time is right, they will release their grip in a safe way and allow the client to do the work they need to do. We know this because these parts are only there to serve the client and to do what is best for them. In fact, we rely on these parts to keep the work we do safe. We work in close consultation with these parts, as we know they will not allow the client to do anything that is not safe for them.

Some of our shadow parts will stay hidden for the whole of our lives and we will still be able to live fulfilling lives and will not be unduly hampered by these shadows. Remember, we put parts of ourselves into shadow in order to survive, and this can still apply in adult life: it may serve us to deny certain aspects of ourselves in order to get by. In Healing The Shadow we believe we need strong motivation to look at the shadow. We don't just explore shadow parts as a sport! The client needs a powerful incentive – for example, because these parts are being destructive in their life or because they sense a vital part of them is missing. Strong motivation is required if we are to take the risk of exploring these shadow places. As practitioners we do not make any judgements about if or when a client explores a shadow side of themselves – we simply allow the work to unfold and are guided by the changes the client wants to see in themselves and their life.

Working with blocks and barriers

Some of us have clear and obvious trauma from our past that casts a shadow over our lives. We can easily see how certain events have wounded us and how our lives are limited because of this. However, many of us have no such overt traumatic memories from our childhood, yet we still carry shadows around with us that are compromising our lives. Such shadows may cause less noise and drama, yet they can still have a significant impact on us: limiting our life experiences and stopping us from acting and behaving in the ways we would like.

Because these shadows are less obvious, they can have even more power over us. We are not aware we are being driven by these hidden blocks and barriers, yet we end up 'sliding off' things we said we would do: we find ourselves staying away from particular situations, we avoid certain challenges, we can't stick to the plans we make. A low level of fear drives our decision-making and we can find ourselves trapped in a life that is smaller and less fulfilling than we would wish.

At Healing The Shadow, as well as working with people who have experienced objectively traumatic or abusive situations, we work with those who wouldn't describe their childhood as traumatic in any way but still received messages and patterns that are not helpful. This work may be more internal and less filled with strong emotion, yet it can be just as transformative as any other work. We talk with the parts that are holding clients back and explore why these first came into being. Through these important conversations, deep change can take place in our psychological make-up. Once these parts have been befriended and understood, they can start to work alongside us rather than against us, and we can then move forward with our lives in a way that is more aligned with our deepest hopes and wishes.

Why all therapists need an awareness of the shadow

The shadow is made up of all the parts of ourselves we have cut off, repressed or denied. We are deeply ashamed of these parts, and because they are so firmly hidden away it is unlikely we will present them to a therapist without an extremely high level of permission and safety.

The Healing The Shadow training gives practitioners the skills to embrace their client's shadow sides as they show up. This allows the client to trust that they can show all parts of themselves in the session, not just the bits that are 'making progress' or 'wanting to heal' or 'feeling positive towards the practitioner or towards the process'. If a therapist is not aware of their client's shadow sides, then these can obstruct therapeutic work.

As explained earlier, in Healing The Shadow we use the idea that we are all made up of many different parts, which all have different thoughts and feelings. Amongst these different sides of ourselves we will find there are some parts that are opposed to each other and are pulling us in very different directions. So we can begin to understand how therapy might be disrupted if the practitioner is not aware of these different parts at play.

For example, if someone comes to therapy because they want more intimacy in their life, there will almost certainly be other parts of them acting against this wish – parts that are terrified of intimacy, for example, or parts that value time alone, or don't trust others, or are unsure of where intimacy might lead.

If a therapist works *with* the client towards their wish to create more intimacy, they will inevitably be working *against* all these other parts. As a result of this, the parts that are frightened of intimacy will be doing everything they can to disrupt the therapeutic process. The last thing these parts want is for the client to create more intimacy in their life! These disruptions can cause confusion, and can result in the therapist feeling like they are battling against their client rather than working alongside them.

Alternatively, the therapist may find they work very effectively in the session in collaboration with the part of the client wanting change, and together they appear to make great progress. Yet when the client returns to their everyday life, the parts that didn't get a voice in the session return even more strongly, obstructing the changes the client is trying to make in their life and undoing all the progress made in the session.

This tension dissolves if we make sure to recognise, encourage and honour all parts of the client. We can then allow the internal conflict within the client to come alive in the practice room. This allows the therapist to facilitate the conflict between the different parts of the client, rather than becoming embroiled in this conflict themselves. Facilitating these conflicting parts to interact directly with each other in a safe way then brings about new solutions, which are integrated into the whole of the person's being.

4.

Discovering What We Have in Shadow

Our shadows, by their very nature, are out of our sight. They consist of parts of us we have hidden away and are trying hard not to see, so either we are completely unconscious of these parts or they are right out on the periphery of our conscious awareness. This means that when we want to explore our shadow side, we have a problem: even though we may have an uncomfortable feeling that there are things hiding away there in the shadows, we have no direct way of knowing what they may be. This is because at some point in our lives we have done an excellent job of hiding them, not only from others but also from ourselves.

Since we can't see our shadows directly, some detective work is required if we wish to discover the parts of ourselves we have hidden away. We can look at this through six different lenses that can each offer us new insights.

What we judge in others

Firstly, we can look at what we strongly judge in other people – the qualities that intensely irritate, annoy or enrage us. When we have a very judgemental reaction to certain behaviours in others, it is likely to be due to the psychological process of projection described briefly in Chapter 1.

Projection involves attributing our unaccepted thoughts, feelings, traits or behaviours to others when they are actually a part of ourselves. Because we have pushed these qualities into shadow in ourselves, we tend to be hyper-aware of them in other people, and when we see them there it bothers us so much we have a strong and judgemental reaction. This is because we can't accept these qualities in ourselves – we believe them to be bad or unsafe – so we don't want to see them in others either. We want to squash them down and shame them in the same way as we have squashed them down and shamed them in ourselves. This process is usually entirely unconscious.

Take the example of anger. If, as a child, I have been told I mustn't be angry or I have learnt that anger is dangerous or hurtful, then I may have decided to put my anger into shadow. I pushed it away, out of sight to myself and out of sight to others. I tried to pretend I didn't have anger. However, as an adult I start to see anger around me everywhere. It really grates on me when other people allow their anger to be expressed – that just seems so wrong! I want to squash it down in them in the same way I squashed it down in myself many years ago. It just doesn't seem acceptable. The point is, if we accepted anger in the other person we would be opening the doorway to accepting anger in ourselves, and this simply seems too dangerous.

Of course, if I have a very strong response to someone who is angry, it doesn't mean the person in front of me *isn't* an 'over-the-top' angry person – they may well be. It just means that it will bother me in a way that it may not bother others who might be able to hold it more lightly. Once I have worked with the shadow of anger and reclaimed a healthy relationship with my anger, I will not be triggered by others getting angry. I may not like it, but I will accept it and understand why they may behave in that way.

In Healing The Shadow we believe that the healthy, clean expression of anger can be helpful to us, the healthy, clean version of every shadow has gold in it for us. If we don't have access to our anger, we can encounter all sorts of problems in getting along in life.

If we notice ourselves judging angry people, it doesn't mean we need to start behaving in extremely aggressive or hostile ways – it just means we may want to look at our own connection with healthy anger. So we can ask ourselves:

Is this something I've lost touch with?

Have I disowned my anger?

Are there times when it might be helpful for me to express my anger?

What's it like to say to myself: 'I get angry sometimes'?

This could be a first step in reclaiming our anger.

The process is similar to other qualities, such as selfishness for example. If we judge selfishness in others, we can enquire into what we might be disowning in ourselves. It's possible that we may have thrown other things away into shadow – by mistake, as it were – along with our selfishness. Putting ourselves first, believing we are important and having a sense of self-worth are all sides of selfishness that we might find missing in our lives. These might be positive attributes we would benefit from reclaiming. So we can ask ourselves:

Am I losing something by denying my selfishness?

Are there times when it would be helpful to be able to put myself first?

Have I lost a sense of my needs being important?

What kernel of gold may I have thrown away along with my selfishness?

What's it like to say to myself: 'I like to put myself first sometimes'?

This kind of exploration can be repeated for any quality or way of being that we find really bothers us in other people. The invitation here is to unpick things in this way – to notice something we really judge in others, ask ourselves if we have cut off that part of ourselves, and if there is anything of value there we might like to reclaim.

What we admire in others

The flip side of looking at qualities we judge harshly in others is to look at the qualities we really admire in other people. Sometimes this is known as the 'golden shadow'. We can project these golden qualities onto others in the same way as we project negative qualities.

Let's take the example of confidence. We may really admire people who have confidence, who can speak up in public, act or sing, or take on a challenging role at work. In our childhood we may have got the message that we were annoying or a nuisance if we spoke up, or we may have been told our gifts didn't amount to much. We may have been told we were too big for our boots or too bossy. One way or another we may have got the message that it wasn't OK for us to be bright and to shine. We put our confidence into shadow in order to get along and be accepted by those around us. So when we see someone else with confidence, we really admire them. We think, *I could* never *be like that… they seem to have something magical that I don't have.* Well, in shadow work we believe we *do* have confidence, that it is a natural part of us all but some of us have hidden it away, and some work will be required to reclaim this part of ourselves.

The invitation here is to look at things we really admire in others and ask ourselves if these are things we have put into shadow. We can then start to own them in ourselves. With the example above, we could try saying to ourselves, 'I am confident, I have gifts to share, people value me,' and see what this feels like. We don't have to believe it right now, but rather just play around with the idea and notice how it feels to speak like this. We can ask ourselves what risks there may be for us if we were to fully own this part of ourselves. This exploration could be a first step towards owning our golden shadow.

People with whom we have difficult relationships

As well as projection, there is another unconscious psychological process we encounter when working with the shadow, and this is the process of transference that was also described briefly in Chapter 1.

Transference is when we start to see another person as if they were someone from our past. We start experiencing them as, for example, our critical father or our neglectful mother. We find them treating us in the same way as this person did, and we start reacting to them in the same way that we reacted to that person. Transference creates a kind of emotional time warp, taking us back to painful childhood experiences, with all their attendant thoughts and feelings. It's important to remember that transference is completely unconscious, and this makes it very difficult to spot and address until we step back to get perspective and to ask ourselves what may be happening. Transference is particularly likely to occur when we face any form of perceived power imbalance in a relationship.

If we look at our difficult relationships, we can explore the messages we are picking up from the other person and then ask ourselves who they might be representing from our past. So first we get a large piece of paper and write down all the messages we hear from the person with whom we are having difficulties. We can then look through the messages and see if we received these same messages from anyone in our past. This can be illuminating work. If we find that a lot of the messages are similar to those received from someone else earlier in our lives, then there may be an element of transference going on in our current relationship, and it may be helpful for us to do some shadow work to explore this past person and the impact they are still having on our lives. We can then begin the process of withdrawing this transference, and we can start to see the current person for who they really are, rather than as a figure from our past.

What we do by accident

Another way we can get an idea of what might be in shadow for us is to notice things we do 'by accident'. These kinds of 'accidents' come about because it's not possible to completely get rid of a part of ourselves. Shadow parts have a lot of energy, and however much effort we put in to squashing them down, at some point they will come bursting up and out – 'by accident'. This usually happens without our deliberate intention – we just can't help ourselves.

However hard we try, at some point what's in our shadow will come flying out. This can be very shocking and confusing for us. It is common to hear people say, 'That just wasn't me – I don't do that kind of thing!' Yet they did, and in shadow work we believe it *is* them, just a part of them they hid away long ago and have lost touch with.

Anger, again, is a great example. If we spend our whole lives trying to be calm and balanced, gentle and thoughtful – not to have any anger in us at all – there will come moments when that is unsustainable. Something has to give. When something catches us off guard we may snap at someone, say something hurtful, or even lash out in rage, immediately regretting it. We quickly regroup and get back in charge of our anger, but the incident is confusing to us. We think, *What happened there? I'm not that angry person!*

Another example could be someone who is happy-go-lucky, never gets upset about anything and is always cheerful. It may be that one evening something doesn't go quite right for them, an event they were looking forward to gets cancelled, or they have an accident and spill something, and they find that this seemingly minor incident has them crying uncontrollably. They find themselves overwhelmed with emotion. They feel silly and embarrassed and don't understand where this might have come from. They may think, *I've got nothing to be so sad about*, yet their overwhelming response suggests otherwise. It's possible that something extremely sad happened when they were young and there was no one around to help them process their grief. It may be that sadness was met with little sympathy in their childhood, or it may even have provoked disapproval or punishment. Alternatively, it may have been their role in the family to keep everyone cheerful, so they had to learn to put their sadness to one side. There are many different ways in which someone may have come to lose touch with their sadness. After so many years of not feeling this side of themselves, they may have stored away a well of grief that feels scary to delve into, it is so unfamiliar. Yet it will eventually find ways to express itself that take the person quite by surprise.

Another very public example of shadows coming out by accident is that of the bride or groom who leaves their intended partner standing alone at the altar. This person may have put all their doubts and fears around being married into shadow and not allowed themselves to acknowledge them. This means they haven't been able to explore these feelings with anybody or work them through. Then the day arrives, and they just find themselves unable to go through with the ceremony, not really understanding why. This happens totally by accident. They would never have planned it this way.

The invitation for this section is to ask ourselves whether a behaviour that comes out by accident could be a quality we have put into shadow. This may be anger, sadness, neediness, fear, arrogance or any other quality. Then, as a first step, to see what it feels like to say: 'I get angry sometimes.' 'I get very sad sometimes.' 'I need other people sometimes.' 'I feel frightened sometimes.' 'I think I know best sometimes.' Or whatever is relevant for us. Reclaiming conscious ownership of these parts of ourselves is a way to start gaining control over these behaviours and to stop them from bursting out by accident.

Leaking through our body

Another way our shadows can leak out by accident is through our bodies. It is usually other people who will notice this, as we are likely to be completely unaware of what is happening. For example, a friend may tell us we look terribly sad, when we ourselves are not aware of feeling sad. Or we may be talking confidently whilst our body language and facial expressions betray our hidden fears. We may be doing our best to be calm and patient with someone, yet our fists may be clenched, demonstrating the anger inside us that has no outlet for expression. These things are beyond our conscious control and out of our awareness. However, if someone does point them out to us, or if we notice them when, for example, we watch a video of ourselves, then we have the option to explore things further.

For example, if my friend tells me I look terribly sad, I could reflect on whether or not there may be something I am very sad about that I have pushed away into shadow. Did something happen, maybe a very long time ago, that I have not wanted to feel? Or if someone tells me I look angry, even though I'm feeling very calm and loving, I could ask myself if there may be anger about some past event that I've never been able to express.

In these explorations it's important to only take notice of what rings true for us. Other people's observations can be helpful, but they can also be clouded by their own shadows and unowned material.

Our bodies may speak out in other ways too – by giving us migraines, rashes, backache or more serious illnesses. It is always worth exploring what unowned part of us might be trying to find expression through our body. Again, it is important that we only listen to our own interpretation of what might be going on.

It is never wise to put too much trust in others' interpretations of our bodily ailments.

Compulsive behaviours

Things we do compulsively can also offer a glimpse into our shadow world. Overeating, smoking, gambling, cleaning – any habit we have that we just can't seem to stop can give us clues as to the unconscious parts of us that are driving things from behind the scenes. These parts of us that we haven't owned can have a lot of influence over our actions.

Consciously, we may want to lose weight and be fit, yet we find ourselves eating automatically in a way we can't control. Here we might want to ask what is going on for this hidden part of us that wants to eat. Is it feeling like it needs nourishing or nurturing? Does it want pleasure, sensuality or comfort? Is it fed up with obeying all the rules we impose? It can be worth taking time to listen to this part and trying to find out what it really wants.

Similarly, if we find ourselves compulsively cleaning, we could ask what it is this part really wants. Does it require order or safety? Does it need a sense of control? Is it a frustrated energy that needs an outlet? Once we become aware of this hidden part, we can then explore how we might be able to meet its needs in a more wholesome and conscious way.

Equally, there may be a pattern we compulsively follow in our interactions with others. For example, we may say yes to everything anyone asks of us, without actually engaging our conscious mind to make a clear decision about whether or not we want to do what they have asked. We may afterwards feel resentment, thinking, *Why did I agree to this?*

Or we may find we compulsively hide. If we are asked to go out, we might find ourselves making an excuse before we have really thought about whether we want to go out or not. Our lives may get smaller without us realising that this compulsive behaviour is limiting our experience.

In situations such as these it can be helpful to take time to reflect on what might be driving these compulsive behaviours. If we can get to know the part of us that always says yes, or that hides, or whatever our habitual response may be, then we can start to understand where this behaviour is coming from. We can listen to what that part needs from us and form a healthy relationship with it so that it no longer needs to drive us in unconscious ways.

Exploration of the above six areas can reveal insights into aspects of ourselves we have put into shadow, and we might choose to follow this by doing some work to explore these sides of ourselves further. This can be challenging and painful work. There are always good reasons for us to have hidden parts of ourselves away. There may have been much pain, fear, shame or guilt associated with these sides of ourselves. Although painful at times, getting to know and accept these parts of ourselves can also be incredibly joyful as we break free from past restrictions and experience the relief of owning and inhabiting the whole of who we are.

5.

The Benefits Of Working With The Shadow

Much has been said in earlier chapters about transformation and the benefits of shadow work – yet transformation is fancy language and a big claim. Whilst there are, indeed, some seemingly magical results to working with the shadow, which can't easily be accounted for in any logical way, I'd like to complete Part One by explaining, as clearly as possible, what we *do* understand about the process of transformation that takes place. I will describe as best I can how this work can have such a huge impact on us, on our lives and on the world around us.

When we get to know a shadow part of ourselves in an embodied way, a change takes place deep down in our psychological system. Over the following months and years, this change ripples upward and can impact every aspect of our lives. As the work integrates into our system, we start to behave in ways we didn't think were possible. We have new resources available to us, we have more energy, better relationships, more confidence and a greater sense of peace and relaxation. We trust ourselves more deeply and we start to see the world around us differently.

In this chapter I'll take each of the eight changes listed in the paragraph above and explain in more detail how we believe this change comes about.

We start to behave in ways we didn't think possible

This happens because we come to know and accept parts of ourselves we have previously pushed away. Because we now accept those parts of ourselves, we can begin to have conscious control over them. This means we get to choose whether or not to act from these parts, and when we do act from them we use them consciously and deliberately and we have control over our words and actions. This brings about significant change in our behaviour, and these parts no longer have the power to disrupt our lives.

As well as letting go of negative behaviours, we also now have access to all the gold and the gifts that were locked away in these parts of us. When we allow ourselves to feel and experience these sides of ourselves, we come to realise that they are not all bad – far from it. There is wisdom in these parts, and they contain resources that can greatly support us in our lives. Because these parts are no longer hidden away, their gifts naturally show up in our lives in new, delightful and unexpected ways.

Once we have access to all this gold, we can start to harness these resources and use them to improve our lives. When Joe eventually went ahead and explored the critical and shaming part of himself with Sam, he found he became a much better parent to his children. He not only stopped criticising them so harshly, but he also began to see where he could support them in their lives and help them to develop. Part of the gold in his critical and shaming part was his ability to see where his sons needed to grow, and to challenge them in supportive ways to do this.

The gold from this part has also shown up at work, where Joe has become a much more perceptive and effective manager.

People appreciate his laser-sharp insight and attention to detail. Now that Joe is embracing his critical side, he has learnt how to use it in service to himself and others and he is finding more and more places where these qualities are welcomed and valued.

We have new resources available to us

As well as finding new resources in the parts of ourselves we have pushed away, we can also explore and develop 'new' parts of ourselves on the carpet, and we can work to consciously and deliberately inhabit these. Remember how Joe inhabited the firefighter's qualities and stepped into the scene to stand up for the frightened little boy? In doing this Joe was able to access a strongly protective part of himself that he hadn't known before, and he was able to develop and strengthen this side of himself in the process. This firefighter part of him has now become an important resource in Joe's life, standing up for him when people behave in bullying or intimidating ways. Joe didn't think it would ever be possible that he could stand up for himself in this way but, since doing the anger work with Sam, he finds he is able to speak up effectively and he no longer allows himself to be treated badly.

Of course, this 'new' firefighter part isn't a completely new part of Joe; rather, it is a part that never got developed during his childhood, so it has felt unformed and insubstantial. As a result of this, Joe has had to learn about this part of himself during his sessions with Sam and practise using it. This is like learning to use a muscle that has never before been used.

We have more energy

It takes a tremendous amount of energy to keep parts of ourselves hidden. We use so much of our life force trying to keep them at bay that we can never be off guard. It is stressful and exhausting. However, once we have brought parts out of shadow, we have freed up all the energy we were using to keep them hidden, and we now have that energy available to us to use in any way we want to. We experience more vitality, and we can consciously redirect this energy to help us build the life we want to live.

We have better relationships

Until we own the dark and destructive parts of ourselves, we will always be judging these parts when we see them in others. Because we fear, shame and reject these parts in ourselves, we also fear, shame and reject them in others. This is the process of projection described earlier. This causes a split with others in our lives and can cause division in society. We can feel isolated and cut off.

We find that once we have accepted previously unacceptable parts of ourselves, we more naturally accept such parts in others. We become less judgemental and more understanding. As we own more aspects of ourselves, we feel more connected to others and more compassionate towards them.

Joe was unable to tolerate the vulnerability of his sons because he was unable to tolerate his own vulnerability. Until Joe accepted the vulnerable, childlike part in himself, he was unable to accept this in his sons and would attack it whenever he saw it in them.

We have more confidence

Once we have accepted a part of ourselves that we judged and pushed away, we are no longer living with the shame of this hidden part. We are then able to accept ourselves more fully and feel more comfortable in who we are.

In Healing The Shadow we spend time working on the carpet with the critical parts of the client that constantly put them down and destroy their confidence. We work to get to know these parts and to find out why they are speaking to the client in this way. Most often, we find they are trying to protect or support the client in some way, but this need for protection is now outdated. In their sessions clients can have conversations with such parts and find ways to 'bring them onside' so that eventually they stop speaking in this critical way and begin to play a more supportive role in the client's life. Our confidence can greatly increase as the critical parts stop attacking us.

As well as this work with critical parts, we spend time developing parts that speak to the client kindly, and that value them and take care of them. This is what happened when Joe brought Ava into the scene on his carpet to support the frightened little boy. Joe inhabited the loving, caring qualities of Ava, and spoke to the little boy from this gentle, supportive part of himself. This felt new for Joe. Because he wasn't spoken to gently and kindly in childhood, he never learnt how to speak to himself in this way. In undertaking this process he developed a part living inside him that can speak to him kindly and gently whenever he is scared or low in confidence. This internal voice makes him feel valuable and worthy and loved. It changes the way he speaks to himself on a daily basis, and this has increased the level of confidence he feels in the world.

We find a greater sense of peace and relaxation

Once we befriend parts that are fighting against each other inside us, we experience a greater sense of peace and relaxation in our system.

Our shadows don't only show up in difficult behaviours in our relationships with others – they also show up as attacking behaviours towards ourselves in our inner world. Our shadow parts can cause a lot of harm inside us because they set us against ourselves. They cause an internal split. This can show up as tension in our body and can cause us to hate ourselves and lead to self-destructive behaviours. We find ourselves confused as to why we can't 'get it together'. This is because we are not 'together'. Inside us a battle is raging. Parts of us are being hated, shamed and attacked by other parts.

In Healing The Shadow sessions we both befriend the parts of us we have been attacking *and* we befriend the parts of us that have been *doing* the attacking. Once we've undertaken this work there is no longer a battle going on inside and we can be more relaxed and at peace with ourselves.

We trust ourselves more deeply

Once we know our shadow sides we can allow them to inform us, rather than needing to push them away. We can come to trust the wisdom they hold. For example, if we have learnt not to like our vulnerability, we may have put it into shadow. Yet this can lead to it bursting out in embarrassing or uncomfortable ways that don't serve us, and we then feel unable to trust this vulnerable side of ourselves. Instead, we push it further away into shadow due to the embarrassment it causes.

However, if we reclaim our vulnerability we can now listen to this part of ourselves rather than shaming it and pushing it away. When we are vulnerable we need support and care, and our sense of vulnerability is letting us know this. Once we learn to accept our vulnerability, we can trust the impulses of this part rather than habitually pushing it away. This means we can act appropriately in situations where we are vulnerable, and we can ask for the support and care we need. As well as this, since we are now listening to the needs of our vulnerable part, it will no longer have to make itself known by bursting out in embarrassing ways that leave us feeling uncomfortable.

In a similar way, if we have pushed away a critical and judgemental part of us, it may come out in cruel and punishing ways that cause harm in our relationships, and so we come to learn that we can't trust that part of ourselves. However, once we've worked with this shadow we can start to listen to that critical and judgemental voice. We're no longer scared of it. If we find ourselves feeling critical of a colleague at work, for example, we can listen to what this critical part of us is saying. Initially it may be saying very unkind and critical things, and we will probably choose not to take these too seriously. But underneath this, if we listen a little more carefully, it could also be saying, 'You really can't trust this person. It's the third time he's let you down. I think you need to challenge him on this and ask him to up his game.' This advice may be worthy of our attention. Our colleague may be grateful for this healthy challenge, and they may work to improve their standards. This could greatly improve our working relationship. Alternatively, if our colleague doesn't rise to the challenge, we can start thinking about what further action we need to take in order to avoid being repeatedly let down by them.

Before we knew these shadow sides of ourselves, we couldn't trust them and we didn't have access to the guidance and wisdom they could offer. We can now trust that there are valuable messages in those parts of us and therefore we can trust our own goodness and value. We can come to understand that even parts we thought were 'bad' are actually there to serve us, and have wisdom to offer us and others if we take the time to get to know them.

We see the world differently

As we undertake more and more shadow work, we begin to withdraw our projections and transference from others and we start to see the world more clearly. We have a better understanding of people around us who show challenging or destructive behaviours, and we feel compassion for them rather than judgement.

For example, Joe used to feel angry and judgemental when he saw stories of refugees on the news in the evenings. He knew he 'should' be understanding of their plight; however, he found himself judging them and seeing them as weak and useless. He didn't like to see or hear about them, and although he knew it was unreasonable, a part of him thought they should just 'sort themselves out' and not be so pathetic. Once Joe came to accept the weak and helpless part in himself and to understand his own struggles and helplessness as a child, he started to see the plight of refugees differently and to have more compassion.

In a similar way, now that Joe knows the critical, shaming part of himself, he doesn't need to project it out into the world around him. When a colleague at work points out a mistake in one of his reports, he can accept her feedback and see that she is trying to help him. He no longer projects a critical stepdad onto everyone who gives him feedback.

Through doing shadow work, as well as understanding that all our shadows contain gold, we come to see another truth alongside this – that all that is golden contains shadow. This brings us a very different view of the world that is far more mature and holistic and helps to keep us grounded and balanced.

What do I mean when I say all that is golden contains shadow? Well, one example might be a relationship that is easy and joyful and full of love and acceptance. This is, of course, something to be celebrated and relished. However, there can be a shadow side to this – the couple may never learn to manage conflict, and may never experience the deepening of trust that comes from managing such difficulties together. Another example might be if someone is the best mum in the world, totally tuned into their children and doing anything for them. There will probably be a shadow side to this too – she may not be looking after her own needs, and she could become resentful or lacking in vitality and enthusiasm for life. If anything is 'too' golden, then it may be that something is being lost or put into shadow to sustain something so amazing. If we grow a wonderful tree, it will naturally create shade underneath it.

So with shadow work we are not aiming for perfection – we are aiming for wholeness and an acceptance and awareness of all that is within ourselves and in others.

Once we have a lived experience of integrating shadow parts, we find we no longer need to see the world in terms of black and white. We can tolerate paradox. We now understand how, for example, someone can love their children deeply and yet at the same time shame and criticise them. We know there are deeper truths playing out under the surface and things can't be taken at face value or understood on a superficial level. We don't feel so much of a need to label things as 'good' or 'bad'. We understand that all parts of everybody are trying, deep down, to do good and to serve that person. We understand from our lived experience that every shadow contains gold and all that is golden contains shadow.

Part Two

The Archetypes

We live in a world that is full of archetypal images. Picture a superhero, an innocent child, a wise elder, a powerful leader. The chances are everyone will produce similar archetypal images as they bring these figures to mind. Whatever our background and our life experiences, these archetypal beings are somehow familiar to us: we have an inherent understanding of what they are like, and vivid images are evoked. In shadow work we find the idea of archetypes to be of great value in providing an intuitive and accessible framework through which we can all communicate and understand our inner worlds.

Robert Bly, in his book *A Little Book on The Human Shadow*, describes us all as being born into a '360 degree personality'.[1] By this he means that we all are born with the potential for the full range of human nature to be expressed in our lives. We are born with the potential of everything it is to be human.

In reality, it is perhaps a little more complicated than this. Given what we know about how much happens in the womb, and the impact this has on the development of the child, it might be more accurate to say we are *conceived* with a 360 degree personality, rather than we are *born* with a 360 degree personality. Even this may not be accurate – it could be that past life experiences mean we are conceived with limitations or constrictions on our personality due to trauma we've experienced previously. However, in Healing The Shadow we find it a helpful idea that our original state is one of full potential, with access to the full range of possibilities for how we could be as a human being. With this whole range of potentialities to choose from, we can live our fullest lives and express our own unique nature.

However, as we know, in childhood we go through a process of hiding parts of ourselves away in order to survive and keep ourselves safe. We put parts of our 360 degree personality into shadow, and this reduces the spectrum of potentialities we can access and depletes our life experience.

But what *is* the full range of potentialities that were originally available to us?

Our work is about wholeness, and if we wish to return to wholeness it is helpful to have a map of what the full spectrum of potentialities might be so that we can start the process of reclaiming these. In Healing The Shadow we find the archetypes offer a helpful way of picturing and thinking about the complete range of human experience and the many different ways of being that are available to us all.

Archetypes can be seen as blueprints that are somehow programmed into every human being's psychological make-up. Carl Jung believed the energy of the archetypes resided in what he called the 'collective unconscious'.[2] In whatever way we understand the archetypes, we find that people intuitively recognise them as part of their humanity. We work with clients of all sexual identities, gender identities and socioeconomic circumstances, from a wide range of cultural and ethnic backgrounds, and we are yet to come across anyone who finds the archetypes do not resonate with them. Everyone tends to have an intuitive sense of the archetypes we use and how these live inside them.

The archetypes are like an internal template from which our individual characteristics are created. They are expressed within us all differently, depending on our particular experiences of life, as well as our own unique inherent nature. The way we express each archetype affects how we interact with the world and the experiences we have in our lives.

Throughout history, people have used many different archetypes to describe the range of human experience, and over the years psychologists have come up with a variety of different names for these. In Healing The Shadow we work with four fundamental archetypes we believe describe the full range of human potential in the clearest and most comprehensive way.

Traditionally, these four archetypes have been known as the Sovereign (the King or Queen), the Warrior, the Magician and the Lover. Many writers have adapted these names and come up with terms they believe better describe the energy in each archetype. In Healing The Shadow we have chosen to use modern names for these archetypes that are gender-neutral and that we find speak to the widest range of people: for Sovereign we use Heart Centred Leader, for Lover we use Feeling Body, for Warrior we use Action Taker and for Magician we use Transformer.

Whatever name is used, these archetypal energies exist within each one of us as separate and distinct areas of our personality, and together they create the whole of who we are.

In Healing The Shadow we work towards the goal of having full and balanced access to each of these four archetypes. Archetypal theory serves as a framework that can guide us in working towards reclaiming this wholeness. It gives us a language to explore our behaviours and how we show up in the world, and it helps us to see what needs to happen in order to rebalance our archetypal energies. The archetypal framework we use can be easily understood by everyone. We find it is empowering for people to have a model they can recognise and make their own. We can all then be fully part of the conversation about the work we would like to do and what direction we want our personal journey to take.

In the next four chapters we dive into each archetype in depth, but for now here is a brief summary that gives a flavour of each archetype and its qualities.

Heart Centred Leader

Our Heart Centred Leader is like a loving parent inside us who guides and blesses us as we travel through life. This is the heart that cares. Our Heart Centred Leader holds the vision for our lives; it is the part of us that knows what we really want, and will encourage and support us as we make our plans a reality.

Feeling Body

Our Feeling Body is the part of us that feels. It connects us with what is going on inside. This archetype connects us deeply to others and allows us to be intimate. This is our spontaneous, creative, dreaming side that enjoys nature, play and sensuality. Our childlike qualities live here, along with our vulnerability.

Action Taker

Our Action Taker is the part of us that can bring about change in our lives and can step out and make a difference in the world. It is responsible for setting our boundaries and saying 'No' and

'Stop'. The Action Taker has integrity and courage and speaks the truth. This is the part of us that protects and defends us, and stands up to injustice.

Transformer

Our Transformer is the part of us that can step back and see things from different points of view. Our Transformer can help us to reframe situations and see things in a new way. This side of us is responsible for assessing risks and keeping us safe. Our intellect lies here, along with our ability to transform our understanding of ourselves and the world.

Looking through this archetypal lens, the aim of our work is for clients to become equally comfortable in each of these four archetypes. We believe that to live a rich and full life we need to have access to all four of the archetypes so that we can call on the one that will serve us best in any given situation.

For example, when having a Sunday morning lie-in our Feeling Body archetype is going to serve us best – being in our Action Taker will not lead to a relaxing morning! However, when asking for a pay rise at work, our Action Taker will probably be the most suitable archetype to be speaking from. When giving a talk at a conference, the Heart Centred Leader is the most helpful archetype to draw on. On the other hand, when in a legal battle with our neighbour, our Transformer will be more appropriate.

Over the whole of our lives, we aim to inhabit an equal balance of all of the archetypes. However, at any given point it may not be possible to express an equal balance of all four. Certain life situations require us to call more strongly on one or more of the archetypes than the others, and we need to accept this when it is appropriate – it is part of the journey of life. For example, illness may call us to be more in our Feeling Body, whilst being a single parent may call us to be more in our Heart Centred Leader and Action Taker. Building a new business may call on us to be more in our Action Taker, whilst studying for a qualification may call us to be more in our Transformer, and so on.

Overall, it is a good idea to look at our lives and consider how we might change things to bring more of a balance of all four archetypes. This sounds straightforward, yet there are powerful reasons why certain archetypes might seem out of our reach. The archetypal theory described in the next four chapters supports us in understanding this. Firstly, we look at each archetype in detail and explore the gifts it has to offer. We then look at why we may lose healthy contact with that archetype and how we can re-establish balance.

In childhood there are certain emotional wounds we can experience that are particularly damaging to us. In the same way that the early messages we received caused certain parts of us to go into shadow, there are some particularly wounding messages we can receive when we are young that can cause us to put a whole *archetype* into shadow. We lose touch with all the healthy aspects of this archetype and instead it shows up in damaging and destructive ways in the form of either inflations or deflations of that side of ourselves. These inflations and deflations can wreak havoc in our lives.

Our work in Healing The Shadow is to heal these emotional wounds and to regain access to the healthy versions of each archetype. We use healing messages to start to bring each archetype out of shadow, and we use processes that give rise to deep, embodied experiences that bring us back into healthy connection with each archetype.

Each archetype is also associated with a core animal instinct. We believe that we have all evolved with animal instincts hardwired into us, yet it can sometimes be difficult to admit this. If we are unable to accept that we have these animal instincts, they will go underground and into our unconscious and this can cause the associated archetype to go into shadow. So part of our work is to integrate and own these instincts so that we can have conscious control over them and we are not cut off from access to the related archetype and all the gifts this may have to offer.

There is also a 'key emotion' associated with each archetype. We see these important emotions as entry points that unlock the gifts of each archetype. We believe we need to be able to access and express all four of these emotions if we are to have access to our full personality. If we find it hard to feel any of these key emotions, then we can work towards freeing up the expression of this in ourselves so that we can regain full connection with the associated archetype.

Once we have freer access to all of the archetypes, we can then use them to express our own unique personality without this being clouded by shadow material that is out of our conscious control.

The archetypal theory described in the next four chapters can give us a sense of which archetypes are strong in our lives and which are absent or under-represented. We may recognise some of our behaviours in the inflations and deflations that are described. This is valuable work, and at the same time it is important to remember that we *all* have imbalances and woundings in *all* of the archetypes. This is human nature, and it is part of being alive and existing in this world. So it is important to focus on how this work can support us in living fuller and richer lives, rather than to spend time 'diagnosing' ourselves in a critical way or judging ourselves for having something 'wrong' with us. We don't hold the position in Healing The Shadow that there is anything 'wrong' with anyone. At core we are all whole and perfect, and this work is designed to support us in discovering and reclaiming this.

7.

The Heart Centred Leader Archetype

Our Heart Centred Leader is the part of us that can step up and take charge of our lives. Our Heart Centred Leader cares about us deeply, supporting us to heal and grow, and inspiring us to fulfil our life's purpose.

Qualities of the Heart Centred Leader archetype in its fullness

Warmth, care and passion

Our Heart Centred Leader is the part of us that loves and cares for us unconditionally and wants us to lead a fulfilling, rich and love-filled life. This side of us is warm and emotionally connected – it is the heart that cares. Our Heart Centred Leader is full of passion and joyfully leads us through our lives. This side of us cares deeply about ourselves and others, and makes moral judgements about how we choose to live.

Guidance

The Heart Centred Leader lovingly guides us towards a life of fulfilment and joy. Sometimes it is helpful to imagine this part of us as an inner loving parent who cares for us and guides us, or as an inner queen or king who rules over our internal realm with tenderness and compassion. They are in charge of our lives and able to create our future, working with the wounds, gifts, strengths and limitations that result from our upbringing and background. Each day our Heart Centred Leader creates the most beautiful, rich and fulfilling day possible.

Heart-led purpose

Our Heart Centred Leader is the part of us that holds a vision for our lives and brings passion and purpose to the way we live. They hold awareness of our mission at this time in our lives – whether this is raising a child, running a company, recovering from an illness, creating a garden, healing others or whatever else we are moved to set our hearts to doing. Our Heart Centred Leader will joyfully and wholeheartedly support us in fulfilling our purpose.

Blessing and supporting ourselves and others

The Heart Centred Leader inspires and encourages us, and also supports us when we are struggling or vulnerable. They are on our side no matter what. This part of us sees our essential value, outside of any achievements or failures. In the eyes of our Heart Centred Leader, we are always worthy of love, respect and care. They are there to support us and to help us find the support and care we need in the world. They are realistic about our abilities and understand that we all need support, that no one manages well in this world alone. It is our birthright to be connected and supported and our Heart Centred Leader will seek out these connections and support networks and recognise us as worthy of this attention and love. Equally, this part of us will support, bless and encourage others in our lives – joyfully and with an open heart.

Feeling gratitude

Our Heart Centred Leader is the part of us that can feel gratitude for all that we have in our lives. We know we are aligned with this archetype when we feel warmth in our heart and gratitude flowing outwards.

Leading and following

As the name suggests, leadership is a key quality of the Heart Centred Leader. This is the part of us that can confidently step up and lead others in a heart-centred way. Yet it is important to realise there are times in our lives when we need to 'follow' rather than 'lead'. This archetype is equally comfortable leading or following – giving or receiving – as is appropriate for each situation.

The alpha instinct

The animal instinct that lies in the Heart Centred Leader archetype is the instinct of 'ranking'; in other words, having an alpha female or an alpha male in the group – someone who leads everyone else, has special privileges and whom others look up to. We instinctively know how to step up and lead when this is called for. Equally, it is in our instinctive nature to be one of the 'followers' at times: one of the lower-level members of the group who looks up to the leader.

If we deny these instincts, then we put a part of ourselves into shadow. It works better to acknowledge that the instinct to lead or to follow is part of us and that human groups may function most effectively when people take on such roles. However, we also recognise that, unlike animals, we have conscious choice. Once we acknowledge these instincts in us, we can choose whether or not to act them out. If we do act them out, then we do so consciously and constructively in the way that best serves us and others.

Listening and speaking

The special role of the Heart Centred Leader is to listen and to speak. This part of us listens carefully to the thoughts, opinions and feelings of others. It also listens to all the different parts of ourselves that may have conflicting or opposing views on a particular issue. Having listened carefully, the Heart Centred Leader speaks their decision and offers their way forward, having taken everything they've heard into account.

Feeling joy

Joy is the key emotion for the Heart Centred Leader. Feeling joy in life is essential if we are to be able to access the qualities of this archetype and embody these. This doesn't mean we're joyful all the time when we're inhabiting our Heart Centred Leader – there may be much sacrifice, difficulty and hard work in leading ourselves and others through life. However, it means we cultivate a foundation of joy and contentment which we can rest in and rely on in difficult times. The source of this joy is a sense of our own worth, beauty and essential goodness. This is a place of self-love, in which we can sit with an open heart. When we know this place of internal joy and self-love, we naturally approach the world with a sense that other people, too, are basically worthy and essentially good.

Having fire in our hearts

We find that fire is a good symbol for the Heart Centred Leader. It represents the warmth and the passion of this place. We say we have 'fire in our belly' or we are 'on fire' when we are full of passion and vision. We say we are 'burnt out' when we have been leading too much, without receiving the support, guidance, rest and nurture required.

Because of this association with fire, we often find it helpful to light a candle when working with the Heart Centred Leader archetype.

Asking openly for what we want

Someone with a balanced Heart Centred Leader will ask clearly and openly for what they want. They know that they will not necessarily get their wishes fulfilled, but they believe that they are free to ask and that their requests will be treated respectfully.

Someone with a wounded Heart Centred Leader will believe that saying what they want is selfish, demanding or humiliating. They will therefore try to express their wants in unclean ways by saying things like 'I really need you to...' or by hoping the other person will guess what they want and then berating them afterwards if they don't get it right. They might feel more comfortable saying what they *don't* want, rather than what they do want. Or they may feel more comfortable saying what they want for other people, rather than saying what they want for themselves.

It is not 'selfish' to want things, nor is it 'demanding'. It is simply a statement of our truth. We all want things. We are all allowed to ask – knowing we may not get what we ask for.

Messages that wound our Heart Centred Leader

There is one type of message which particularly harms our ability to embody our Heart Centred Leader. This is the message that we are 'not good enough' in some way: that we need to try harder or improve ourselves or 'do better' before we will be accepted and loved.

If we have picked up this message in life, from our parents, family, community or teachers, it will eat away at the foundations of our joyful loving of ourselves. It plants the belief that we have to strive and prove ourselves if we want to be loved. It sends the message that we are not worthy of love and care just as we are: that we will be judged and compared with others, and if we are found lacking in some way, love or approval will be withdrawn.

This is sometimes known as conditional love.

This wounding message can be received when a parent is experienced as betraying us in some way. This experience of betrayal is at the core of the Heart Centred Leader wounding – when those who were meant to love us wholeheartedly have betrayed this unwritten agreement. This may be, for example, a parent leaving the family, dying, killing themselves, sending us to boarding school, being obsessed with work, emotionally absent or highly critical. Or it may be that we were required to perform in some way in order to receive a parent's love. There are many different ways we can receive the message that we are not good enough for those around us.

Shadows of the wounded Heart Centred Leader

If we have been wounded with the idea that we are not good enough in some way, then our Heart Centred Leader will be wounded and will show up in unconscious shadowy ways that we don't fully understand.

Inflated behaviour

It may be that we 'puff up' to try hard to prove how good we are. We chase success after success, showing off and being proud of our certificates, medals or accolades. Yet deep down we still fear that, without these badges of honour, we are worth nothing. So we continue trying to achieve – more and more – and it becomes an endless cycle, which never gets us the love and acceptance we are looking for. The more successful we become, the more we fear we would be nothing without our success.

Alternatively, we may try to prove our worth by caring for and serving others relentlessly. However, rather than receiving love for this, we are more likely to be taken for granted by others and tossed aside when they no longer need us. Even if this isn't the case, we will always fear that if we weren't so caring or supportive we might lose the love and high regard of others: we believe we need to be performing in some way to get their love.

We may find we judge people who don't seem to achieve anything much, and who get love and support simply for being themselves. We see such people as weak and useless. This is because, deep down, we are jealous of people who are loved *just* for being themselves. We have put our longing for unconditional love into shadow, so it is painful for us to see others receiving this.

Deflated behaviour

Another reaction to the belief that we're not good enough could be that we totally deflate. We collapse and give up. There is no fire in our heart. We think everything's too hard; we feel tired and don't believe we will ever achieve anything. We can feel depressed and unmotivated and may feel there is no point to life.

We can become jealous and vindictive when we see powerful leaders, or when we see people living the life of their dreams. We have cut off this side of ourselves and put it into shadow – so we judge it harshly in others and can think they are self-centred or arrogant or 'too big for their boots'.

Many people who are wounded in this archetype alternate between inflated and deflated responses.

Messages that heal our Heart Centred Leader

The messages we need to hear in order to heal our wounded Heart Centred Leader are:

You are good enough just as you are.

You are worthy.

You are perfect just the way you are.

You are perfect for me.

I love you just the way you are.

I love and accept all parts of you.

It can be very powerful to hear these messages spoken directly to us, whether this be from a friend, partner, family member or therapist. However, sometimes actions speak louder than words, and we can receive these messages just as effectively through people's ways of being around us and their behaviours towards us. This can be equally healing.

The healing processes for the Heart Centred Leader archetype are designed to convey these messages of acceptance and love in a powerful way that brings about change deep inside us. As this change takes hold and embeds within us, it starts to heal our Heart Centred Leader wounds.

Healing processes for the Heart Centred Leader

Support

We find that support is the key to developing a healthy Heart Centred Leader. In our society, nearly all of us have received the message, in one way or another, that we need to do things on our own, that there is some kind of badge of honour in doing things without the support or help of others. Our education system encourages this, with endless testing and a lack of encouragement to admit weaknesses and to collaborate with others and share responsibility. So on a very simple level nearly all of us are wounded in this archetype, and we would benefit from receiving more support and from being given more permission and encouragement to get that support.

When we were children, many of us had times when we desperately needed support and it wasn't available. We can see this from Joe's story: in his childhood he didn't have any support available to him when his stepdad was physically and emotionally abusing him. His stepdad's abuse didn't happen in isolation – it was part of a time in his family life when his mother was very vulnerable, both financially and emotionally, and was not in a place where she could give Joe the support he needed.

When children don't receive support, their confidence and belief in themselves starts to waver. They begin to doubt their worth: surely, if they were worth anything, then those around them would be there to love and support them. A child needs support in difficult times in order to make sense of what they are going through, to express their feelings and to understand that what is happening is not their fault. They also need support in order to know and believe that they are worthy of support.

So the main process we use to heal Heart Centred Leader energy is bringing support onto the carpet and into the client's inner world – just like Sam brought in Ava to give support to little three-year-old Joe. Please note: it is the client who chooses this healing process for themselves, not the practitioner. We find that clients naturally choose the piece of work that is right for them at the time, just as Joe chose, in his session, for little three-year-old Joe to receive some support. The session is always guided by the client, and they have full choice of the work they want to do. This ensures that the work done is the right work for the client and that the session is following their agenda and is tailor-made for them.

So the client may have a vulnerable, childlike part on the carpet that they want to support, or it may be a frightened, confused, shy or intimidated part. This process works effectively for any part of the client that could benefit from support and care. To bring in this support, we create a new part of the client that can really love and care for the part that needs it. This new part may be an adult part of the client, or it may be an external person – one of the client's friends perhaps, or a spiritual being, or a fairy godmother – anyone who has the qualities needed to give the support required.

The client then steps into this part, inhabiting this supportive energy and speaking to the part on the carpet that needs support. They will do this in whatever way feels right for them – it will depend on what kind of support is needed – and the client themselves is the person best placed to know this.

This process of bringing in support grows the client's Heart Centred Leader energy. They are embodying their own inner parent or carer, a part that can support them when things are hard in life. This part isn't only there during the session – its energy has now been activated and will remain inside the client. From there it will continue to speak kindly and supportively to the client outside the session, in their everyday lives.

Now, many of us know that sometimes it is not so easy to find a supportive part of ourselves that will speak kindly to us, and this is also true during this process. Sometimes, however much the client wishes to speak lovingly to the part that needs support, they may find themselves being critical or shaming instead, and unable to find the supportive place in themselves that they were looking for.

When this happens we see it as a powerful, unconscious part of the client that has taken over in that moment. So we will step the client out and back to their seat and we will read out the messages that this 'supportive' part said so that the client can watch the scene from the outside. From this place they will usually be able to see that this isn't the kind of support they really want. On hearing the words back, people often recognise them as the words of a critical or shaming person from their past. Without realising it, they have been continuing to speak to themselves internally in this unkind way, even though that person is no longer in their life. Or sometimes people discover that they started to talk to themselves in this way during difficult times to help themselves get through. Such parts can be trying to help us to 'do better' for our own wellbeing and survival, yet they do this in very harsh and critical ways. This may have been necessary many years ago, but now it is outdated and unhelpful.

So there are a variety of different reasons why we speak to ourselves in critical ways, and clients can start to get insight into this as they hear back the words that were spoken. Speaking critically to ourselves is often an unconscious process that operates outside of our control. Once the unkind voice has been made conscious, it is usually possible for that part to quieten down and allow other parts to speak. Because it has been brought out of shadow, it no longer has the power to take over and dominate the process. The client can then step into a truly supportive and caring side of themselves, and they will find this easier to access now that the other voice has been heard and recognised for what it is. They can then bring wholehearted support to the vulnerable part, speaking lovingly and kindly and bringing tenderness and care.

So through this work the client accesses a part of themselves that can be supportive and loving. However, for the work to be complete the client needs to *receive* this support as well as to give it. Having a wounded Heart Centred Leader is just as much about not being able to receive support as it is about not being able to offer it. The next step is for the client to feel the impact of hearing these supportive words and to fully take them in.

For this second step the client is invited to step back into the vulnerable part that is in need of support. They will put the cloth back on and settle back into the feelings of this part. They can then make contact with the cloth of the support person – they may want to hold it, like holding someone's hand, or they may want to wrap it around themselves, like receiving a hug, or they may just want to look at the cloth and picture the person there speaking to them. The practitioner will then read back the words the supportive part said and the client can now receive these words and take them in. This completes the support loop, and gives the client the experience of receiving the support they never had.

Acceptance

Many of us have parts of ourselves we struggle to accept. We can often shame these sides of ourselves, treating them with disgust and contempt. This is damaging to our Heart Centred Leader, as it means we are not able to love the whole of ourselves – we only love the parts that have our approval, and other parts are rejected by us.

We can bring acceptance to parts in a similar way to bringing in support. When the client has identified a part of themselves they find hard to accept, we can work to bring acceptance to that part. We can look for a part of the client or an external person who *would* be able to fully accept and understand that part. The client then steps into this place of acceptance, wrapping a cloth around themselves and taking on the qualities of acceptance and understanding that this part has. They then spend time speaking with the part that has not previously been accepted, and forming a connection with it. They show understanding for this part and why it is there, and they welcome it into their inner world.

To complete the process, they then step into the place of the part that hasn't been accepted, and they receive these accepting words and messages from the supportive part. These words can begin to heal the pain of their rejection and allow them to take their rightful place as a recognised part of the client's inner world.

Visioning

As well as working with support for vulnerable parts, we work with the parts of clients that have vision and hopes for their life. These parts can need recognition, support and encouragement if they are to have the confidence to bring their visions to fruition. So another way we heal the Heart Centred Leader archetype is by celebrating clients' achievements in life so far and supporting them in their vision for their future. We will invite them to inhabit a part that holds ideas and hopes for their future, and we will hear and celebrate these with them. Celebrating and encouraging our clients' hopes and aspirations is a very important aspect of the work we do. This work is not simply about healing wounds – it is also about accessing the gold that has been hidden away and supporting and encouraging people to go out into the world and create the life they want to live.

Integration

The Heart Centred Leader is the part that can hold and accept all other parts. It is therefore key to bringing about integration within us. When we have two opposing parts on the carpet that cannot find any agreement, we will look for a Heart Centred Leader part that sees the good in *each* of these parts and accepts and welcomes them both. This part will then speak to the opposing parts one at a time, offering understanding, blessing and acceptance. Over time, this work helps the client to accept and integrate different parts of themselves and to feel a greater sense of wholeness and ease.

Nia – a client with a Heart Centred Leader wound

Nia is a successful and wealthy entrepreneur who owns a chain of high-end health and beauty stores. Alongside this she is the CEO of a children's charity in Central London.

Nia sought out her practitioner Meera for support due to difficulties in her relationship. After many difficult conversations with her partner, Jeff, about having children, he had threatened to leave her. Whenever they talked about starting a family together, Nia would agree to the idea in principle but would always find an excuse as to why it wasn't the right time. Usually work commitments would get in the way – the next big project would be just about to start, or a conflict within her team would consume all her time and attention. After ten years of waiting, Jeff had given her an ultimatum: agree to start a family in the next year or I will leave.

The truth was that Nia lacked confidence around being a parent. Despite being hugely successful at work, when it came to close relationships she didn't feel she had anything to offer. She believed that parenting would be too hard for her and she wouldn't be able to do it. She thought she would fail, so she didn't want to try: without the trappings of her 'work' persona, she didn't feel she was worth anything.

Nia had covered this up with excuses about needing to work and not wanting to lose focus, but underneath this she was terrified. Work was a place where she could be guaranteed to be seen as successful, so long as she worked hard enough. At home it wasn't the same. She felt exposed and as though she had nothing to offer and no worth. She didn't understand why her partner stayed with her, other than because she brought in the money. Giving up work, even for a short amount of time, terrified her. She didn't know who she would be without it.

This is typical of a Heart Centred Leader wound. Either a person is working tirelessly to prove they are 'good enough' or they collapse completely and don't even want to try. They are unable to simply rest in themselves and to believe that they are good enough just as they are.

Nia was always reluctant to reach out to others, and when Jeff threatened to leave her, even though she was devastated, she found it extremely uncomfortable to think of turning to anyone for support. She never asked for support in her life, quite the opposite: she was identified with the role of supporting, coaching and leading others. Yet she was terrified of losing Jeff, and she didn't know how to work through the difficulties they were having without outside help. A friend recommended Meera as being one of the best in the field, so Nia took a leap of faith and began to attend sessions.

With Meera, Nia was able to verbalise the fears and insecurity she felt around starting a family. This was the first time she had ever put these feelings into words, and talking about it all felt very vulnerable. However, Meera's careful, warm and non-judgemental listening put her at ease and she began to relax.

As they spoke, Nia came to realise that she had taken on a lot of uncomfortable messages from the people around her about what it was like having children. These messages didn't come from anyone in particular, but more from the whole of society. Although no one had ever said these things to her, she imagined she had picked them up from people's behaviours and certain comments they made. So Meera suggested they got a whiteboard out on the carpet to represent 'society' so that they could then write up all the messages Nia had heard and explore them further. Nia thought this was a good idea, and so they got to work together.

Nia chose to place the board right in the middle of her carpet, and she picked out a golden cloth to place over it. Meera asked her what messages she heard from 'society' and she wrote them up on the whiteboard:

You have to be the best mum ever.

It's impossibly hard but you have to do it.

If you fail you won't be forgiven.

You have to do everything on your own.

There is no support.

You can never make a mistake.

You have to be better than others.

Just being yourself isn't good enough.

Others can take it easy, but you have to be exceptional.

Meera asked Nia if she ever heard these messages anywhere else in her life and Nia realised she had heard something similar from Jeff – not quite the same, but she believed he wouldn't forgive her if she wasn't a good mum and that it wouldn't be

OK if she asked him for support; she would need to manage it all alone.

Under Meera's care and guidance they then started to explore the root of these messages. Meera asked Nia when she had first heard or experienced messages like this. This question took Nia back to her childhood and she began talking about her father and some of her early experiences with him.

Nia had been very close to her father when she was a child, and he thought she was amazing. He always praised her for her academic ability and sharp mind. He would allow her to stay up late whenever she had exam successes, and this was a real treat. When she was thirteen and passed the entry exams to a prestigious school, he invited her into his office for a brandy and she had never felt happier. On the surface, the messages she received from her father were ones of blessing and praise:

You are my amazing girl.

You are highly capable.

I celebrate your success.

I know you will go far.

However, as she explored this more deeply with Meera, she found that beneath these surface messages were some more uncomfortable messages that had caused her a lot of fear and had put her under considerable strain:

If you fail I won't love you.

You have to do everything on your own.

You always have to try harder.

You have to be better than others.

Just being yourself isn't good enough.

Other children can play and relax but you can't.

These were the messages that had caused an emotional wound for Nia. She loved having her father's approval, and yet she constantly had to strive to achieve it. She couldn't ever relax, and she feared that if she failed she would lose his love and be of no worth in his eyes.

Nia was surprised to see that the messages she received from 'society' were almost identical to those she had received from her father. She began to understand that the messages she had heard from her father were still playing out in her life today. They coloured her perception of herself and those in her life. This is why she assumed that if she failed, Jeff would no longer love her and she would have to do everything on her own and be better than all the other mums.

She realised she projected these messages onto others without questioning or exploring if they were really what other people were thinking. She also realised she said these things to herself *all* the time. She told herself no one would ever love her if she failed at things. This is why she worked so hard. It was not only because she believed in the work she was doing, but also because she simply couldn't be seen to fail. She imagined that if she didn't succeed in her work, she would be left utterly alone and unloved.

The messages from 'society' that she had placed at the centre of her carpet were essentially the messages she had received from her father. So she was now seeing this golden part in the middle of her world as representing her father. This felt more accurate. Although the exact wording of some of the messages was different from those she had received from her father, the overall impact was the same. Nia realised she had lived her whole life in fear. She saw that as a little girl she had been terrified of losing her father's approval and being rejected by him. She never rested, she never played. She worked hard all the time to impress him, and she lived for the brief moments of recognition she received.

She saw that this frightened little girl still lived inside her and was terrified of making a mistake and losing the love and approval she had. When Meera asked her what she would like to do next, she chose to step in and explore this frightened child part of herself. She chose a pale green cloth and placed it just in front of the message board that was in the centre of the carpet. When she stepped in to wear the cloth, she sat looking at the messages feeling very tense and scared. She spoke for a long time with Meera about how she had felt as a child: how much she loved her father and how hard she tried to impress him with many sleepless nights spent studying in her room alone.

Following this work they had a break and a cup of tea and surveyed the scene on the carpet. In the centre was Nia's father and his messages. Just beneath these was the pale green cloth representing Nia as a child, desperate to keep her father's approval.

Nia decided she wanted to bring in some support for the little girl. So she stepped into a part of herself that felt compassion for that child and how hard things had been for her. She went to speak to the child and to bring her some care and support in what she was going through. However, this was not straightforward work. The part she stepped into said:

It's OK, I'll support you in getting things done, you just need to be more organised. Sometimes you just need to try a little bit harder and be more disciplined. We can do it together. It's important to please your father, he only wants the best for you.

When Nia heard these words read back, she realised they were not quite the kind of support she wanted. In a way, they were only gentler versions of the messages she had received as a child from her father, and they still called for her to work extremely hard and gave her no permission to rest or play. It still felt like there was no room for failure. This is what she had grown up believing love looked like, and when she was in the support part it was hard for her to think of anything else to say other than these messages she knew so well.

Meera then asked her who she thought they could bring in who would be truly unconditionally loving and supportive to the little girl. Nia closed her eyes and chose an angel. A large, golden, loving angel with big wings and a kind face. When Nia stepped in to become this angel, she spoke to the little girl quite differently:

My precious one, I see how frightened you are. You don't need to worry. You don't need to worry about anything. I love you however you are. It's OK with me if you fail. It's OK with me if you want to rest. You are a child, you should play. I don't want you to have to worry. I am here. I can look after you. You don't need to do anything at all. Just relax, just be yourself. You are lovely just as you are. I will always be here for you, I will never leave, I am here for you no matter what.

Nia stepped into the place of the little girl and wrapped the golden wings of the angel around herself whilst Meera read out the words the angel had said. Meera put on some music and gave Nia time to take in these new messages. Nia's body softened as she soaked up the healing from the angel's words and allowed them to land deeply within her.

8.

The Feeling Body Archetype

Our Feeling Body is the part of us that holds our ability to connect deeply. It is the vulnerable, trusting, creative and playful side of us that is relaxed and able to go with the flow of life.

Qualities of the Feeling Body archetype in its fullness

Connection to all

The Feeling Body archetype is *all* about connection. This is the part of us that is capable of deep connection – both with ourselves and with others. This part of us connects to our feelings and allows them to flow and be fully expressed. Someone who is in touch with the Feeling Body archetype lives in constant connection with their body – they enjoy their body and are sensual and sexual. They also connect with others easily and share themselves with openness and vulnerability. This part of us connects with nature, with the universe and with spirit. This archetype is connected to the flow of life and is spontaneous, creative, imaginative and carefree.

Vulnerability

When we are in our Feeling Body we are open and defenceless. This can be an intensely vulnerable place to be – think about how exposed we are whilst making love or sharing our deepest emotions. In order to inhabit our Feeling Body safely, we need to develop a strong, protective side to ourselves that can create safe spaces for us, where we can take the risk of exposing our vulnerability. We need to find people in our lives who will protect and care for us when we are vulnerable so that we can relax and be held safely in this tender place. The Feeling Body is certainly not an archetype that can survive alone. This part of us knows no caution and is undefended.

Yielding

Our Feeling Body holds our capacity to trust and rely on others, and is able to receive without needing to give anything back in exchange. We can think of this as 'giving the gift of receiving' to those around us. When we are well cared for, we learn in the first few years of our lives that our very existence is a gift to those around us, and that looking after us and giving us what we need is a joy to our parents and carers. From this, we conclude that we are intrinsically valuable and lovable – and that yielding to another person's love and care is a beautiful and safe way of connecting.

So when all goes well in this area we learn that we are loved and lovable, that it is safe to rely on those around us, and that we have a right to openly receive their love and care. If all doesn't go well in the first few years of our lives, our Feeling Body archetype will not be able to fully develop in a healthy and trusting way.

Connection with our physical body

As the name suggests, our physical body is integral to the Feeling Body archetype, and we need to be connected with our physical body if we are to experience the gifts this archetype has to offer. Our emotions are experienced as sensations in our physical body – this is why they are called 'feelings'. Sensual and sexual pleasure are also experienced in the body. Our experiences of safety and trust are felt in our body as a sense of warmth and comfort and relaxation.

Trauma responses from the past are also held in our bodily tissues as 'body memories'. So trauma lives in this archetype too, along with the potential for healing that trauma and releasing the traumatic memories from our body.

The innocence and pain of the Inner Child

The Feeling Body is the place of our Inner Child and carries all the vulnerability, innocence and openness of our childhood. Since our body holds the memories of our trauma and distress deep in our tissues, it also holds our traumatised Inner Child in this way,, who can be seen as living in our body, awaiting the time when these overwhelming feelings can receive the love and healing they need.

Connection with what is happening under the surface

The Feeling Body connects us with others in an unspoken way. Many studies have shown that our ability to understand someone else's emotional experience depends much more on non-verbal communication than on verbal communication.[3] In fact, the vast majority of what we know about another person's emotional experience comes from tone of voice, body posture and gestures – all of which are the territory of the Feeling Body archetype.

Whilst two smartly dressed business people may appear to be having a serious, unemotional, 'grown-up' conversation during a meeting, at another level there are also two inner children having a conversation with each other, without the adults even knowing about it! Indeed, the outcome of the meeting may even be determined by this 'hidden' conversation, without either of the participants really understanding what has happened.

This simple example demonstrates the power of the Feeling Body archetype. This is the archetypal energy that drives many of our choices and decisions, without us necessarily being consciously aware of it.

Our physical bodies carry out many activities over which we have no conscious control: regulating our heart rate, digesting food, healing physical wounds, releasing hormones and so on. There is a whole world of life-giving activities that go on unseen inside our bodies, and this is a good illustration of the often unconscious, non-verbal, intangible yet essential nature of the Feeling Body archetype.

The need to bond with others

The animal instinct in the Feeling Body archetype is the bonding instinct. When we are born we are almost totally in our Feeling Body, and the other archetypes haven't yet developed in us. A child's first and most urgent instinct as a helpless baby is to bond with its mother. Their very survival depends on it. The Feeling Body archetype helps us to do this: it's programmed to try and connect with other people from the moment we appear in the world. The power of this drive is immense, yet it's not consciously felt by most people. Even so, it controls much of what we do and how we are in the world as adults. We are social animals, and when we don't have the opportunity to meet others and connect with them on a social level, we may descend into mental disorder and lose touch with reality.

Connecting with others

The role of the Feeling Body is to help us connect. The openness, vulnerability and softness of the Feeling Body are intensely connecting qualities. However, the Feeling Body does not connect with others by 'helping' or 'supporting' or 'caring for' them. The Feeling Body connects by 'being with' them. This part of us connects through a deep listening and quality of attention, through emotional presence and perhaps through physical touch or simple actions. The Feeling Body can connect in a way where no words are necessary and when there is nothing helpful that could possibly be said.

In the purest form, this archetype is not trying to make things better for someone, or trying to improve them, or to take away their pain. There is no agenda. There is no 'doing'. There is just presence and connection. This is the quality of connection that some of us feel when we are 'in love', which is why this archetype was historically known as the 'Lover' archetype.

Feeling grief

Grief is the emotion that opens the door to this archetype. Feeling our grief – a natural response to loss of any kind – allows us to feel our vulnerability and makes us aware of our simple human need for connection. Grief can shake us to our core and may destroy any image we have of being 'independent' or 'strong'.

Grief puts us in touch with our overwhelming need for connection with others. It also puts us in touch with our inability to control the world and what happens in it, and the need to yield and accept our vulnerability in life. When we grieve fully, we can learn how to live with the losses we have experienced. This brings a new openness that allows us to move on and form new, healthy and joyful connections in our lives.

Being in the flow

We find that water is a good representation of the Feeling Body archetype. In this archetype we are willing to yield to life's flow and to be taken wherever it leads. We associate water with this flow of life, often referred to as the 'river of life'. When we are inhabiting this archetype, we feel 'in the flow' and our lives seem to flow easily and naturally without us needing to force anything or fight anything. We relax in our bodies and allow ourselves to experience everything life brings us.

Water also represents the bodily nature of this archetype, since our bodies are made mostly of water and water represents the tears we shed when we grieve. In addition to this, water can take us under the surface to where the Feeling Body operates, pointing to the unconscious nature of many of our interactions and the sense of our lives being driven by strong undercurrents, over which we have little, if any, conscious control.

Sharing our emotions openly

Someone with a healthy connection to the Feeling Body side of themselves is very happy to openly share their emotions.

They will say 'I'm so angry with you' or 'I'm so very, very sad', and their body language will be congruent with what they are saying; they will look angry or they will look sad when they say such things.

However, when we are wounded in our Feeling Body, we might find it hard to say what we're feeling directly. We might say 'I rather wish you hadn't left me last night' instead of 'I felt angry when you left me last night'.

Alternatively, we may attribute feeling when we are discussing something factual. We may say 'I really feel like we are going to run out of money soon' rather than 'The bank account is very low. I think we will run out of money soon.' What we actually feel is probably fear or anger, but we are either not in touch with this feeling or not comfortable expressing it.

Messages that wound our Feeling Body

The messages which wound the Feeling Body archetype are messages about our ability to love or be loved. In essence, they are anything which makes us believe that somehow we don't love in the 'right' way or that we're not lovable. We can't trust connection or our ability to connect.

This wound around not knowing how to love is often caused by painful loss or rejection when we are very young. If we pick up these messages early in life – from our parents or siblings, or indeed from anyone with whom we look to bond – they can stop us opening ourselves up to others and looking for connection in a natural and unforced way. These messages take away our innocent trust in what we feel and how we want to connect. They replace our innocence with doubt, uncertainty and self-judgement.

Shadows of the wounded Feeling Body

If we have been wounded by the idea that we aren't capable of loving properly, or that we're unlovable, then our Feeling Body archetype will be wounded and will show up in unconscious shadowy ways we don't really understand.

Inflated behaviour

Maybe we start trying really hard to show how loving we are and how well we can connect. We may become intensely emotional and demanding of attention – gazing deeply into people's eyes, touching or stroking them and being overfamiliar in ways that cause others to feel uncomfortable.

We may live a life of drama, going from one emotional crisis to another. This can sometimes annoy other people, as they sense, quite rightly, that the emotion is not entirely genuine – rather, it is an unconscious attempt to 'prove' how emotionally connected we are. However, what we are not connected with is the deeper pain that is driving us – the pain of the belief that we can't love and aren't lovable.

Our overwhelming need for connection, underpinned by the belief that we may never get it, can drive us to look for connection in damaging or dangerous behaviours, such as addictions to food, alcohol and drugs, or the use of sex or pornography. We can also become addicted to work, social media, fitness and many other activities that don't, on the surface, appear damaging. However, because these addictions and self-soothing behaviours simply cannot offer the true human connection we are looking for, our deeper needs are never satisfied, and so we keep going back to these behaviours, needing more and more of the same 'fix'. This drive lies behind the compulsive nature of many addictions.

Our wounded Feeling Body can also show up in the physical body through flashbacks or post-traumatic stress episodes – these are strong bodily emotions and responses that are unrelated to what is going on in the present day. There is often a lot of drama in the life of someone whose Feeling Body energy is inflated, and this level of dramatic emotional experience can seem unnecessary to the outside observer. When this archetype is out of balance, it can also reveal itself through the body in the form of illness, bodily pains and tensions.

Deflated behaviour

On the other hand, on receiving these wounding messages, rather than displaying this compulsive need to connect and the intense overreactions linked to this, we may 'deflate' in our Feeling Body archetype and collapse completely. We may come to believe that we will never be able to give and receive love, and we might decide to give up entirely on this aspect of our lives. We may become very stoical, dry and unemotional. We may defend ourselves from further hurt by adopting a pretence, a façade of neither needing nor looking for love. We may judge and look down on people who are strongly connected to their Feeling Body, and we might shame people who are emotional, sexual or vulnerable, and find these aspects of human nature quite distasteful.

Messages that heal our Feeling Body

The messages we need to hear in order to heal wounded Feeling Body energy are:

You are a deeply loving person.

You are lovable.

I enjoy connecting with you.

I enjoy loving you.

I enjoy being loved by you.

It is wonderfully healing to hear these messages from friends, from our partner, from family or from a therapist. However, given that the Feeling Body archetype is more about feelings and sensations than words, it can be even more healing to receive these messages via someone's way of being around us: seeing their eyes light up when they meet us; having them seek out our presence and spend time with us 'just being'; having them stroke and hold us; and having them joyfully receive our overtures of love.

The healing processes for this archetype are designed to convey these messages about our ability to love and be loved in an embodied way that brings about change deep inside us. As this change takes hold and embeds within us, it starts to heal our Feeling Body wounds.

Healing processes for the Feeling Body

The Feeling Body archetype is wounded by the belief that we don't connect in the right way and we don't know how to form connections or that we can't trust connection, either with ourselves or with others.

Even though it may not seem obvious, we believe that the capacity to connect with others is directly linked to the capacity to connect with ourselves. Many of us struggle to connect deeply with ourselves. It may be that sensations in our body are simply too overwhelming for us to manage: we can't trust them, and they feel dangerous for us. Or it may be that our emotions are experienced as overwhelming and capable of causing harm to ourselves or others. Such experiences, of our body being an unsafe place to be, mean we can start to avoid connection with ourselves and our body, pushing this away into shadow.

In addition to this, when we are wounded by receiving these painful messages around how we love, we may develop negative associations with love – we may hide away from love, avoiding it at all costs, or we may look for love in all the wrong places, resulting in addictions or in painful or unsatisfactory relationships.

The Feeling Body processes address both the wounds around connecting with ourselves and the wounds around connecting with others.

Hidden Loyalty

Even though we may have picked up messages in our lives around not knowing how to connect, the truth is that we are, and always have been, deeply connected. We are deeply loving beings – it is our nature. When we lose someone we are close to, we will naturally find ways to stay connected with them and their memory. We may have a place where we keep beautiful things we associate with them and photos of the two of us together. Or we may have activities we undertake that remind us of that person – fishing, shopping or reading – something happy that we used to do together.

However, if we lose someone painfully, this natural grief process gets interrupted. With complicated and painful loss, we don't have the simplicity of happy memories. We may even want to block out much of what happened in the relationship. This can lead us to believe we are not a loving person.

Unconsciously, however, we are still driven to find a way to stay connected with this person, because this is our nature: we are *deeply* loving beings and we connect at any cost, even with those who have caused us pain. What this means is that we are likely, without realising it, to have taken on something painful as a way of staying connected to the person we have lost, rather than allowing ourselves to lose our connection with them.

We may take on our mother's pattern of alcoholism as a way of staying connected with her, or we may take on our father's criticisms of us and drive ourselves relentlessly, never content with our achievements. We hold tightly to these patterns, as they are all we have to keep us connected with the person we have lost. Yet we do this unconsciously, without understanding what is driving us, and at the same time holding the belief we are not loving or lovable, or that we didn't love them enough.

The truth is quite the opposite: we loved this person so much we were willing to take on something deeply painful, just to stay connected with them. In Healing The Shadow we call this painful connection a Hidden Loyalty. It is a way we are staying loyal to that person and our love for them, yet it is hidden from our conscious awareness.

So one of the processes we use for the Feeling Body archetype is a process that releases this Hidden Loyalties wound. However, we don't only suffer grief when we lose people we love, we can also experience grief around any loss – of a homeland, a job, a pet or our health, for example. This process works for any kind of grief that hasn't been fully processed.

However, for simplicity, here we will look at the process in terms of the loss of a person.

The first step is to support the client in grieving fully for their loss. A representation of the person is brought onto the carpet and the client can go and be with them and speak to them and tell them everything they have been carrying since they left. Then, having released all of this emotion, the client can, with love, put down the painful pattern they've been carrying and give it back to the person they've been carrying it for.

Giving back this pattern will, however, leave an emptiness in the client. This pattern was the only thing keeping the client connected with their loved one, and without any other way of staying connected to them the emptiness will be too overwhelming to bear. The client will simply pick up the painful pattern again – that is how strong their love for this person is. They will stay connected to them no matter what – however painful it may be.

So, to support the client in letting go of their old way of connecting, we will help them to look for a new and more joyful way to keep the memory of that person alive. We take time to discuss with them the qualities of the person they have lost, and any memories or anything warm or joyful associated with that person they would like to hold on to. In this way they find a new pattern of thinking and feeling that they can take away with them as a way of staying connected with their loved one. With this new bond in place, they are much less likely to fall back into the old and painful pattern.

This beautiful and tender process can bring an end to decades of suffering for the client, allowing them to let go of painful patterns they have been carrying for many years. Just as importantly, this process also helps them to understand that they *are* a loving person, and that they have been demonstrating this love by carrying this painful pattern for such a long time. Fully grieving in this way gives the client a new identity as someone capable of loving and connecting, and it allows them to go on and form new and joyful connections in their life.

Inner Child work

We also bring healing to the Feeling Body archetype when we speak to vulnerable, childlike parts of the client on the carpet. We welcome and support the client's vulnerable Inner Child, and this gives the child a voice and the confidence to reach out and look for the love and connection for which they are longing.

Inner Child work is a significant part of the work we do in Healing The Shadow. Our childhood feelings, fears, angers and sadnesses have often been shamed and put away. This means most of us have an Inner Child part that is unacknowledged, unloved and uncared for by us, and is hidden away in the shadow.

Without receiving the attention they need, this Inner Child can rule things from behind the scenes, driving us to look for connection in unhealthy ways, such as addictions, toxic relationships, overeating or any other behaviours that go some way towards giving the Inner Child the sense of connection and nurture they long for.

Rather than pushing the Inner Child away, we find it is much better to befriend our Inner Child and consciously give them time and attention, even though we may initially feel uncomfortable with some of their needs and wants and their high level of dependency. This way, if they have their needs met, they will no longer be driven to disrupt our lives by ruling things from the shadows. More than this though, as we welcome them into our lives we can start to reclaim some of the golden qualities the

Inner Child carries – playfulness, tenderness, creativity, innocence and trustfulness, to name just a few. The Inner Child carries our connection to much of the joy and wonder of life.

We work with the Inner Child by stepping the client fully into that child part of them on the carpet. This is like the work Sam did with Joe when he was speaking to his scared three-year-old boy. We will spend time just 'hanging out' with this child, giving them our time and attention in a gentle, non-intrusive way. We will find out about their life and what it is like: what they fear and what they long for. This is like giving nutrients to a dying plant. To 'feed' the Inner Child in this way transforms the way they feel about themselves. It brings them back into the fold. They can come out of hiding and be loved and cared for by the practitioner in the therapeutic space. Through this process, they can start to take their rightful place in the client's life – bringing more vitality, joy, love, connection and deep feeling into the client's world.

Metaphor work and trauma work

This work is about the client's relationship with their body and their inner world. We work with strong feelings and sensations in the client's body as a way of bringing the client into deeper connection with themselves. There are many different ways to do this work, depending on what is happening for the client.

We support people in learning how to be with overwhelming feelings and sensations inside them. We assist them in staying present with these strong feelings, allowing them space and time. They can then learn how to make room in their body for these feelings, allowing them to flow whilst also remaining connected to the practitioner. We invite the client to explore the messages these feelings carry and to listen to them, rather than trying to push them away. We work with metaphor to help the client picture what is happening in their body so that they can start to name and understand what is going on inside them and become more familiar and comfortable with this.

Trauma is perpetuated when we are unable to be with overwhelming feelings in our body. We either lash out at others as a way to avoid these feelings, thus creating more trauma and pain in our lives, or we re-experience trauma as a result of the intensity of the feelings going on in our body, which can be terrifying and quite overwhelming for us.

But why do some of us feel such intense and distressing sensations in our bodies? This is to do with the body's ability to shut down in response to intense fear and trauma. Intense feelings can get trapped in our bodies when we undergo an extreme type of 'freeze' response that continues for an extended period of time, with no opportunity for the original frightening event to be processed. This occurs when we are in a situation that we find terrifying and where we are unable to defend ourselves or get away, and there is no support available.

In such situations, all the feelings associated with the event, such as rage, terror, confusion and helplessness, become trapped in our bodies. Because they are unable to flow, these feelings don't get resolved in the way the body would naturally 'wish' to do. Our rage doesn't get to fight, and our terror doesn't get to flee. Nor do we get to express any grief associated with the event. If we don't get the opportunity to process these feelings and express them in an externalised, physical way, we will continue to carry them around, 'frozen' inside our bodies.

However, at some point later in our lives, when we feel safer and are more supported, we can begin to 'unfreeze'. We begin to re-experience some of these overwhelming emotions and the frightening bodily sensations that go with them. These bodily sensations can include irregular heartbeats, palpitations, sweating, shaking, breathlessness, choking, the inability to breathe, digestive issues, stomach ache, diarrhoea, the buzzing of nerves, a fuzzy head and visual impairment. They can often give us the sense we are going to die, or that we are going mad.

Touching back into such intense emotions and frightening bodily sensations can cause a person to go back into a state of 'freeze' due to experiencing a sense of overwhelm and panic. So the trauma persists. The person again hides the feelings away and they remain locked in the body.

As adults, the energy held in these bodily emotions is just as strong as when it was first trapped there. But there are two differences now. First, the original threat is long gone. Second, as adults we are more likely to have the resources we need to support ourselves through these feelings and sensations, whereas in childhood we did not.

As well as running powerful emotional processes in Healing The Shadow, we also believe an important first step to healing trauma is to share with the client these beliefs we hold about trauma so that they have some understanding of the idea that their trauma might be stored in their bodies. This helps clients understand that their extreme fear reactions to current-day situations may be based on historical experience rather than on the current situation. They can then have more compassion for themselves and the way they react to certain situations, and they can gain an understanding as to why certain pieces of work might help them in their recovery.

Much scientific research has been done to verify this idea of trauma being stored in the body. Peter Levine is one of a large number of authors who have written extensively about this and his books are a great place to start to find out more about this fascinating subject.[4] Many people find it helpful to discover that there is a scientific explanation for the trauma responses they are experiencing in their daily lives and that they are not going mad, nor are they about to die – they are simply re-experiencing terrifying sensations and feelings from a past event.

These feel very real because they *are* real sensations in the body – yet the event that originally caused these sensations is in the past. Whilst we might have been in real danger of dying from the original threat, we won't die from feeling these sensations now.

A trauma spiral occurs when a person becomes frightened of feeling frightened, and so never explores the sensations long enough to find a resolution. This information about the science of trauma can help to interrupt the trauma spiral and give the client belief that there is a way forward, where they can learn to allow and heal from these overwhelming emotional states.

Working with the roots of addictions

When we receive the message that we don't love and connect in the right way, we will often start to believe that we need 'too much' of something. It may be we need too many cuddles or too much of people's time, or that we talk too much or require too much attention or too much care. When our overtures of love and connection are rebuffed, we start to believe there is something wrong with us for wanting this kind of connection. We begin to believe that it is simply not possible to receive as much as we are asking for. We come to feel shame for our 'neediness' and we hide it away and stop reaching out for love.

This tends to lead us to finding other ways to get this need met that give us moments of relief from the pain we are carrying. It may be food or video games, reading or other hobbies. We may look for love in dangerous places and end up getting hurt – either physically or emotionally. As we get older, it may be drugs or sex or work that fills this hole for us. If we find something that works, we are likely to go back to it again and again.

This can lead to addiction, where we form a dependency on a drug or a certain behaviour or habit because it gives us a sense of connection and safety. We have finally found a reliable way of getting our needs met without having to face the shame, rejection and pain of a deep relationship.

The problem here is that we cannot substitute for human love and connection. So whatever we have chosen will never really fill that hole. This is why we feel the need to go back again and again and it is never enough. With deep human connection, we know when we have had enough and we move away, knowing we can come back any time we need more. With an addiction though, we never get this sense of having had enough, because it is not filling the real need. So we keep having to go back for more and we end up in a cycle of dependency, which can be damaging and can prevent us from finding true connection and intimacy in our lives.

In Healing The Shadow we work with clients to understand the roots of their addictions. Once they understand the childhood wounds that drive their addictive behaviours, they can work with those wounding scenes on the carpet. They can help the little child to know they were not 'too much' – it was simply that those around them were unable to meet their needs. They can come to understand that they were always loving and lovable and their need for connection was natural and healthy. They can have an experience on the carpet of taking as much time and attention as they want, of never being told they are 'too much', of talking for as long as they want and receiving all the connection and attention they crave.

This work can start to heal the wound they have been carrying and, having received the love and care they need in a therapeutic space, they can eventually allow themselves to take the risk of looking for this kind of connection in their outside lives. With this true connection in place in their lives, the hold of addictive behaviours will weaken and they will no longer have to look to these to get their needs for connection met.

Lyra – a client with a Feeling Body wound

Lyra came to Theo for sessions because of her difficulties in finding a relationship. She was lonely and didn't feel like she belonged in the world. Lyra had been in very few relationships, all of them short-lived. She had all but resigned herself to never finding someone she could share her life with when she came across an article about shadow work and resonated with some of its ideas. One day, when she felt particularly low, she contacted Theo and started a series of sessions.

Lyra wanted to find out more about the sense of loneliness and isolation she felt. She knew many people loved her, and she had people around her who she knew would care for her and support her if she asked – yet she never reached out to them. She had suffered many periods of depression in her life but none of her friends were aware of this. At a deep level she didn't believe anyone would ever really be there for her.

When Lyra was born her mother was suffering from severe depression. Although her mother did everything she could to show her new baby love, she was never really able to give Lyra the kind of holding, care and attention she needed. She would ignore her cries and leave her alone for extended periods. As a child Lyra 'gave up'. She was not demanding or attention-seeking, she simply retreated into her own world, knowing she would never get what she wanted from her mother. She became very independent and dreamy. She didn't do well when she first started school and felt lost in the playground, not knowing how to connect with others and feeling somehow set apart from what was going on around her. She felt desperately unhappy but didn't know why. She had a family who were there for her, fed and clothed her, took her on holidays and gave her as many toys as she wanted; she didn't understand what was wrong. The truth was that although her mother was no longer depressed, Lyra was still unable to find comfort and connection from her. They both tried to be close, but something was missing.

Lyra was anxious before starting the work with Theo. She had been told by several friends that she was distant, reserved and unemotional, and that she should 'get in touch with her feelings'. Also, her last partner had ended their relationship, saying Lyra was too independent and never shared what was going on for her. Because of these criticisms, she was concerned that Theo may have expectations of what the sessions should be like and that she wouldn't be able to fulfil them; she was worried that she might be expected to come up with dramatic shows of emotion and she didn't feel she had it in her. She felt shame around her difficulty in feeling and she didn't want to be put under any pressure to share what seemed so inaccessible and private.

So in her first session Lyra was greatly relieved to find that Theo had no set ideas about how she should be or how they should use the time. Quite the opposite; he seemed only to be interested in Lyra and her experience, wanting to follow her wishes and explore the parts of her she wanted to explore. He clearly had no agenda for the session and no wish to do anything other than understand Lyra as best he could and to be by her side as she traversed her inner world.

Lyra liked Theo and was pleased to find that she felt relaxed in his presence and able to be herself in a natural way. They worked together for many sessions and Lyra's sense of safety deepened. They spent time getting to know Lyra's inner world and the different sets of thoughts and feelings that ruled her life.

In the first session they spoke with a part of Lyra that simply didn't trust other people and refused to allow her to let down her guard and look for connection. In the next session they explored a part of her that felt shame around her difficulty in connecting with others. Over time they also spoke to a harsh, critical part of Lyra that believed she was a failure and not able to get anything right, and they spoke to another part that believed she was unattractive and unlovable.

It was healing for Lyra to explore these parts of herself that had never previously been given a voice. For the first time in her life, she was sharing her inner world with another human being. At the same time, she was starting to connect more deeply with herself and to really understand the emotional challenges she faced.

In a pivotal session, they discovered a part of Lyra that was refusing to let her feel *any* emotional pain. This part had developed when she was very young, and had protected her from feeling the overwhelming despair and hopelessness of not being able to connect with her mother. Lyra named this part her Protector. Her Protector had looked after her as a baby and a young child by taking her attention away from the pain she was feeling. This protective part encouraged her to self-soothe with soft materials and cuddly toys, and to look to books, music and nature to find comfort.

The role of this part was to numb Lyra out, to distract her, to calm her – whatever was necessary to avoid the pain. Her

Protector felt strongly that it wasn't safe for Lyra to feel her feelings, and saw it as her job to do whatever was necessary to prevent this.

As Lyra came to know all these different parts of herself, she could see how they had developed in her early life to help her cope with the situation into which she had been born. Things started to make more sense. Through this process, she began to feel more compassion for herself and to better understand the difficulties she was experiencing in her life.

After several months of working with all these new parts, Lyra told Theo she would like to explore the infant part of her that had experienced such a lack of touch and care when her mother was depressed. Theo suggested that before starting this work it might be a good idea to discuss it with Lyra's Protector part. Lyra agreed, and when they spoke to the Protector part it expressed concern, wanting to make sure the work would be done in a way that was not too overwhelming for Lyra to manage.

After several conversations between Lyra and her Protector, the Protector agreed that it was OK for her to step into this infant part in the therapeutic session, with Theo looking out for her. The Protector part could see that this might be healing for Lyra but also wanted to ensure Lyra wasn't in that space for too long. So they set some boundaries around time and agreed that initially they would spend just five minutes exploring this part. They also agreed on a signal Lyra could make to let Theo know if it felt like too much and she wanted to come out before the five minutes were up.

When she stepped into this part of herself, she found it was a quiet and motionless place. There were few words, as the feelings were largely pre-verbal, but when it did speak, this part of her expressed a sense of loss, confusion and fear, and a sense of hopelessness that was overwhelming.

Theo and Lyra worked together to find a way of supporting this very vulnerable part of her. It wasn't easy work, as the infant simply didn't trust the support parts they brought into the scene. In the end, rather than a person or being, they brought in a large oak tree, with big low-down branches. This finally brought a sense of safety to the young part, and Lyra was able to picture herself resting in the branches, being held and feeling safe in the 'arms' of the tree. In the next session they also brought in a mother bear, who lay in the tree with little Lyra, holding and gently stroking her.

With this sense of safety in place, Lyra began to feel more sensations in her body when she was in the baby part. She began to feel a trembling inside her, which she initially felt some shame about and tried to suppress. When Theo noticed this trembling, he encouraged Lyra to allow the movement that her body was trying to make. She started shaking strongly and weeping. Theo encouraged her to allow the sounds that were coming, and she found herself crying out, full of fear and anger. She beat on the carpet with her fists and Theo gave her a cushion so she could express this anger safely. She said that she hated her life and she continued to shake. Eventually Lyra's body settled, and she began to cuddle in again with the mother bear. Her breathing calmed down and she felt relaxed and peaceful.

With the sense of safety that the tree and the bear brought to her, and with Theo's loving presence, Lyra had been able to connect with the depth of despair and rage she had felt as a baby and as a young child. Despite appearing to be a placid child, Lyra had suffered serious emotional distress due to her mother's depression and inability to connect with her. Now, she had been able to express some of that feeling for the first time and release it from her body. However, it was not just the expression of these emotions that was healing – it was doing this *in connection* with Theo, trusting him and feeling safe enough to share this with him. This was a significant step in Lyra's healing and the start of her learning to take the risk of connecting more deeply, both with herself and with others.

The Action Taker Archetype

Our Action Taker is the part of us that stands up and protects us. It gives us our sense of power and agency in the world and takes the action needed to bring about change in our lives.

Qualities of the Action Taker archetype in its fullness

Protecting and defending

The Action Taker is the part of us that protects and defends us – it is on our side and is able to put us first. This is the part of us that holds our boundaries, stands up for us and says 'No', 'Stop' or 'This isn't OK with me'. The Action Taker protects our vulnerable Feeling Body archetype and creates a safe space for us in which we can live, love, learn and grow.

A sense of power and agency in the world

The Action Taker is the part of us that takes purposeful action to help us achieve our goals. This is the part of us that can make a real difference in the world and it enables us to move through obstacles that inhibit our growth. This archetype takes the action necessary to bring about the wants and the desires of our Heart Centred Leader, and will work tirelessly for a chosen cause or to protect and defend those more vulnerable than ourselves.

Accountability

The Action Taker holds us and others to account. When we break an agreement or behave in a way that has a negative impact on others, this archetype will take responsibility and will make amends by taking the action needed to put things right and repair the harm done.

Truth speaking

The Action Taker is solid, reliable and trustworthy, and is courageous in facing difficult situations. This is the part that stands up for what we believe in. The Action Taker has the courage to speak the truth. Even when it is not popular they will speak truth to power, and will stand up for those more vulnerable than ourselves.

The territorial instinct

For the Action Taker archetype, the animal instinct is that of claiming, marking and defending our territory. If we ignore this instinct, we put a part of ourselves into shadow. It is better to acknowledge that this instinct is part of us and that there may be some benefits to be gained from listening to this side of ourselves. Once we acknowledge this, we have a choice about whether or not we act from this place. Sometimes we might choose to act in territorial ways; sometimes we might choose to be more open.

Feeling anger

The key emotion for each archetype is the emotion we need to be in touch with, and capable of feeling, in order to unlock the door to this side of ourselves. Being connected to our anger is essential for us to fully access the Action Taker archetype and to embody this part of ourselves.

Anger is like a strong message that comes up inside us, telling us that something is not OK: a boundary has been crossed; a commitment has been broken; or something is blocking our growth.

If we are not in touch with our anger, then we have no warning sign to tell us when our boundaries are being crossed. Our Action Taker needs to be alerted by our anger so that it can step up and take whatever action is required.

Anger also gives us direct access to our power. It provides us with a surge of energy. This gives the Action Taker the strength necessary to follow through on whatever needs to be said or done to make the situation right.

Sometimes the Action Taker can do nothing to change the current situation. In such times it is possible to harness the energy of the anger to help us move forward in a different direction and to grow more fully into who we want to be. For example, imagine a person gets unfairly dismissed from their job and feels a huge amount of anger about this. They then discover there is nothing they can do to right the wrong. So rather than setting themselves a futile task, their Action Taker can choose to channel their anger, and the power it gives them, into finding a better paid, more fulfilling and more enjoyable job – maybe even into changing career and finding the job of their dreams!

Being grounded and trustworthy

We find that the earth element is a good symbol for the Action Taker. The earth – in the form of stones and rocks – is solid, strong and never-changing, and this represents the trustworthy, reliable nature of the Action Taker. Earth, in the form of soil, represents the willingness of the Action Taker to 'get their hands dirty' – to deliver unpopular messages and to make difficult decisions.

Setting clear boundaries

Someone with a healthy Action Taker will clearly and firmly set boundaries and let others know when something is not OK. This is done without any sense of blame or need to punish. It is simply a clear statement of what's not OK with them. For example, 'It is not OK with me that...' or 'It doesn't work for me when...'.

Someone with a wounded Action Taker will find it hard to make such statements. They will find endless disempowering thoughts coming into their head, such as:

> *They're not meaning to be unkind. They can't help it. We've been friends for ages. They'll be so upset. They might not take any notice. They might get angry. I might make things worse. It's not a big deal. I'll say something next time. It might be kinder not to mention it.*

And so on. Anything to avoid confrontation!

Of course, the irony here is that this doesn't have to be seen as confrontation – it is merely being clear about our innate right to express what is not OK. Many people can find it very helpful when we express our boundaries clearly, although there may, of course, be some who find this difficult.

Alternatively, someone wounded in their Action Taker may set harsh or punishing boundaries, shaming or blaming the other person. These are usually ineffective and only serve to cause fear and harm in relationships.

So, as you can see, a wounded Action Taker finds it hard to put themselves at the centre of their life and to speak from a place of potency and power.

Messages that wound our Action Taker

Messages that harm our ability to embody our Action Taker take away our right to exist and to be who we are. There are several forms of this wounding, any of which we may take on as a belief about ourselves. One is the message that we don't exist, another is that we don't (or are not allowed to) exist as a separate individual, and a third is that it is not OK for us to be who we truly are.

If we picked up these messages early in life – from our parents, family, wider social community or our teachers – then we will find it very hard to take any action that impacts the world. These messages take away any sense that we matter. We end up believing that we have no right to put ourselves first, nor to protect and defend ourselves, nor to grow.

Shadows of the wounded Action Taker

If we have taken on the idea that in some way we don't exist, or that we're not allowed to exist as we are, then our Action Taker will be wounded, and this energy will show up in unconscious shadowy ways we don't really understand.

Inflated behaviour

If we have a sense that we don't exist, then we may 'inflate' to try and prove that we *do* exist. We may pick battles just so that we can get a sense of fighting and winning. We may enjoy meeting someone in conflict and pushing up against their boundaries just so we can feel ourselves as 'real'. For if we can affect another person, then we are confirming to ourselves that we really do exist.

We might hold to very tight boundaries and be inflexible, 'stonewalling' others and not listening to their opinions, thoughts or feelings. We may 'flatten' others with the strength of our opinions and our need to be 'right', to be 'the winner'. At worst we can be bullying and abusive in our forcefulness.

Alternatively, we may try to prove that we exist by achieving something huge and having an impact on the world. Or we may seek a clear identity by 'bigging ourselves up': driving a high-end car; having a loud stereo; adorning ourselves with expensive branded goods; aligning ourselves with successful teams or TV personalities; or assuming an identity that impacts others – a formidable boss, gang leader and such like.

If our Action Taker is wounded, then our anger, one way or another, will have gone into shadow. We will have decided at some point in our lives that our anger was dangerous, either to ourselves or others, or that it didn't serve us in some way. When anger is repressed into shadow, its energy does not simply go away. As Robert Bly memorably said, emotions put into shadow 'de-evolve towards barbarism'.[5] The anger simmers away just below the surface. So when repressed anger does emerge, perhaps under intense provocation or stress, it can come out unexpectedly as rage – violent and out of our control – doing far more damage than clean anger could ever do.

Deflated behaviour

Another reaction to the message that we don't exist could be that we totally deflate. We absolutely believe in our lack of presence, power and potency. In fact, we have no sense that life could ever be any other way. We don't even try to protect ourselves, and we may allow ourselves to be walked over as we accommodate others' invasions, insults, abuse and denigration to our own detriment. We may become a martyr to others and feel like a victim.

If we believe we have no power, we may not keep our commitments – either to ourselves or to others – and people will probably think of us as 'flakey'. We may avoid conflict. We may have formed the belief that we don't need anger, or that we don't have anger, or that anger is bad or undesirable. But really, our anger goes underground and, because we are not expressing it in 'clean', 'clear' ways, it comes out in passive-aggressive or manipulative behaviours that can be infuriating to those around us and damaging to our relationships. Deflated anger may also emerge as sudden violence, although that is usually directed at ourselves or objects around us rather than towards other people.

Messages that heal our Action Taker

The messages we need to hear in order to heal our wounded Action Taker energy are:

I see you.

You matter.

You are important to me.

You have a right to be exactly who you are.

It can be very impactful and healing to hear these messages spoken directly to us by others. However, the Action Taker is about 'doing' not 'saying', so what will be most impactful for us is to receive these messages through the actions of others. People can demonstrate these messages to us by respecting our boundaries, listening to us when they have upset us, honouring agreements with us and standing up for us in difficult situations.

Healing processes for the Action Taker

Setting a boundary

Clients who've been emotionally wounded in the Action Taker archetype will not know how to effectively set a boundary, whether this is saying 'No', telling somebody their behaviour is not acceptable or stating clearly what they don't want. If we have been given the message that we don't exist or that we don't matter, it will naturally follow that no one will listen to us or respect our boundaries. So work on the carpet is necessary to give us the opportunity to practise this essential relationship skill.

By providing our clients with the opportunity to get in touch with their Action Taker energy and to practise setting a boundary in role play, we offer them the opportunity to learn, in a safe space, what it might feel like to embody this energy in the outside world. As the client learns how to assert and stand up for themselves in this way, they will begin to believe that they *do* exist and that they *do* matter.

When the practice of verbally setting a boundary is combined with physically embodying Action Taker energy, our clients can experience a new state of being they can take back into the outside world. They can begin to see real-life differences in the way people listen to them and respect their boundaries. This will continue to build their Action Taker archetype and affirm their existence and importance in the world.

A simple but extremely effective way we support a client to step into their Action Taker energy is to teach them the phrase 'It's not OK with me…'. Using this phrase in a role play setting can give clients a powerful experience of using their Action Taker energy to set a boundary.

In this work, we assist a client in staying with the discomfort they may experience as they learn how to be assertive. For example, even something as simple as saying 'It's not OK with me that you spoke to me like that' can be a risk for many people – it may go against everything that life has taught them, and saying it, even in role play, may evoke fear, discomfort, shame or guilt. Helping the client to find a strong, clear statement they can really get behind makes all the difference when they are learning how to speak up for themselves and set boundaries.

There are two important aspects to the phrase 'It's not OK with me' that make it something the client can get behind and say with confidence. When we pay attention to both these aspects, it really helps the client to access their Action Taker energy.

Firstly, the words 'with me' are essential to the process. These words change the phrase from being a judgement about the other person having done something 'wrong' to being a statement about the client and what they themselves don't want or can't cope with. It allows for the possibility that the same behaviour may be OK with another person, but it's not OK *with me*. This means there is nothing for the other person to argue or disagree with, as we are not making a statement about *them*, we are making a statement about *ourselves* and what is not OK with us.

Secondly, the statement works best if it is completed with a fact and not with a judgement. It doesn't work well to say, 'It's not OK with me that you are so ignorant and illiterate.' This just comes across as an insult and is not empowering to say. It is also pointless to set a boundary around something so nebulous and poorly defined, as the other person is unlikely to get a clear message about the behavioural change we are asking for.

The Action Taker's job is to bring about change. To this effect a statement such as 'It's not OK with me that you spelt my name incorrectly' would be a much better Action Taker statement. The other person then knows and understands what is not OK, and if they choose to they can take action to change this.

So we encourage clients to complete their statements with a fact that the other person could agree with. They are then on solid ground with what they are saying. They have a strong and clear statement they can get behind and they are less likely to get knocked off course. This is important, even in a role play situation when the other person isn't physically present. It is difficult to embody Action Taker energy if you cannot fully get behind what you are saying and know it to be true for you.

Examples of good Action Taker boundary statements are:

> *It's not OK with me that you haven't paid back the money you borrowed.*

It's not OK with me that we spend our weekends apart.

It's not OK with me that you speak to me like that.

It's not OK with me that you drink in the evenings.

It's not OK with me for you to comment on my body.

Once the client has found a strong statement, we can then work with them to help them speak this statement in a powerful and effective way.

Sometimes it can be helpful to express anger towards a symbolic representation of the other person in whatever kind of messy way it comes out so that we can explore and see what this feels like. It can be a very impactful experience to be given permission to do this, and we may gain some sense of having been heard. However, using 'It's not OK with me' can deepen the exploration.

Using 'It's not OK with me' adds something different; it gives us an empowering statement that we can really stand behind and say in a strong, embodied way. Simply expressing 'messy' anger or rage and insults can sometimes leave us feeling impotent or overwhelmed. Using 'It's not OK with me' can work well as a follow-up to speaking anger in a more free-flowing way. Using this phrase will leave us feeling stronger and more confident, with an effective tool that we can take away and use, as appropriate, in our real lives.

This is *inner work* that is done in an energetic and symbolic way. However, our experience in the room strengthens our Action Taker energy. As a result of this, we will naturally start to set appropriate boundaries in our lives when it is safe to do so.

Using full anger work to bring about a change on the carpet

We have a belief in Healing The Shadow that the Action Taker is a very embodied part of us and that we can most effectively get in touch with this energy by using our bodies and doing something physical. This is nothing to do with violence against another person – it is about having an embodied experience of our strength and power of intention. It is about getting to a place where we physically experience ourselves as having the energy and power to make a tangible difference in the world.

When a client chooses to express their anger in this way, we find the safest method is to use a foam bat and a large cushion. Alternatively, boxing gloves can be used so that they can hit the cushion with their hands. It is also very helpful for clients to use their voice, and to be able to make as much noise as they wish. We often play loud music whilst they do this, as it gives them a kind of 'permission' to raise their voice or shout without inhibition.

Action Takers need to see a result in exchange for their efforts if they want to gain a sense of their power and agency. So we don't generally encourage people to step in and express their anger without also offering them the experience of bringing about a tangible change in front of them. This work often involves standing up to someone who has had a negative impact on our lives. Once we have the messages we received from this person represented on the carpet, we can then stand up to these using the force of our words and our anger. The practitioner can then remove the board from the carpet as we do this work so that we see the messages leaving our inner world and experience a result in response to our effort. For many people who have known anger to be dangerous in their lives, this is the first time they get to experience the safe and effective use of anger, where no one gets hurt and there is a positive outcome.

In this work it is not the person themselves whom we are removing from our inner world – it is the messages that person's behaviour sent to us and the negative impact these messages are having on us. We saw a version of this with Joe, when he used the anger of the firefighter to drive the messages from his stepdad off the carpet. This work gives the client an experience of standing up for themselves and seeing something happen as a result. With this experience, they are building their sense that they can set boundaries and make a difference in the world, and that they exist and they matter. They learn they no longer need to be impacted by those damaging messages.

Much of our time working with anger is spent exploring the barriers that are experienced when it comes to expressing this anger, as this is not usually an easy or comfortable thing to do. People who are wounded in their Action Taker carry a great deal of fear around anger and its possible negative repercussions. We have tools we employ to work with the fear, resistance and sense of disempowerment that can arise. This deeper preparation allows people to access their anger in an empowered and uninhibited way, and for the work done to be fully integrated.

Breaking through something

Sometimes, rather than simply getting rid of people and their messages from their inner world, a client may wish to 'break through' messages that are stopping them from reaching a desired goal. This is a very powerful way to work with Action Taker energy.

We simply find something to represent the desired goal (this may be a loving relationship, a promotion at work or anything else the client is wanting) and we place the representation of their goal at the far end of the room. Then, in front of the goal, blocking the way, we place the messages that they need to break through in order to reach this goal. This is creative work and can be done in many different ways depending on the situation. One way or another they will do anger work with each of the messages, one at a time, and when they feel more powerful than that message they can remove it, tear it up or cut through it. This way they move steadily forward until they reach their goal. They can now claim this as a new part of their life, having found the energy and power to stand up to all the messages and blocks that were in the way.

Giving something back

The dynamics of struggling families often involve one particular individual carrying a certain type of energy that other people in the family don't want to feel or own. This is colloquially named the 'hot potato', and it's often a transgenerational phenomenon, which means the family's 'hot potatoes' bounce down the generations from person to person and land on a particular individual each time. In psychological terms this is a form of projective identification.

Projective identification happens when family members project various thoughts, feelings and behaviour onto another member of the family, who then begins to assume an identity associated with those projections. They take on the projections and believe them to be true, acting and behaving as if this were their identity, and not understanding that they are carrying the unwanted thoughts and feelings of others in the family. It's easy to see how a person with weak or non-existent boundaries could be the victim of projective identification.

As someone becomes clearer about where they stop and others start, they can begin to reclaim their own identity. We can assist them in this work with a process of 'handing back' qualities that were never theirs in the first place. This can be symbolised by using cushions or cloths to represent the qualities or identities that need to go back to their rightful place. Action Taker energy can then be used in the form of the bat and cushion to lend power and meaning to the act of symbolically breaking away from these unwanted identities. The client can then hand back one cushion at a time to the person or people they came from, and they can simultaneously say words that are appropriate to the situation. Again, a considerable amount of energy can be generated in this process, and this can be cathartic and healing for a client as they fight for a truer sense of their own identity.

Cutting the cords

Sometimes we can maintain connection with people who have been harmful to us. Many of our clients will have had the experience of entering into relationships that have gradually become more toxic and damaging. And even if a client has managed to physically end such a relationship, there can still be lingering resentment, fear and even emotional attachment based on the negative and destructive aspects of the relationship. This may persist long after the physical relationship has ended.

Using Action Taker energy, we can help people to symbolically cut these lingering connections or 'cords'. Without such attention, these cords may persist, usually to the client's detriment. Such attachments are, after all, simply another method by which people give their power away. And whilst it's true that many people write about 'cutting cords' as a spiritual process, we can see it simply as a symbolic process of reclaiming power, separating from another person and establishing a clear boundary around our own life and identity.

There are many ways to symbolise this on the carpet. As with other Action Taker processes, a combination of physical activity that has a visible result and of words that express the client's intention can be a powerful external representation of an internal change in that person's way of seeing their world.

Reclaiming something

It follows, as you can imagine, that a client with weak boundaries may have had certain qualities taken away from them by other people. On the carpet, we can offer them an opportunity to reclaim these qualities.

In one sense, all Action Taker work is about reclaiming power. But we may have lost many other qualities besides our power. Some obvious ones that come to mind are: the freedom to speak; the right to be who we are; the right to be seen; the right to be heard; the right to be sexual; the right to be masculine or feminine... The list is almost limitless.

Action Taker work can symbolise the reclaiming of these qualities. All that is needed is a representation of the person who has 'taken' these qualities, perhaps holding some cushions or cloths to represent what is to be reclaimed, and a symbolic way in which the Action Taker part of us can recover what is rightfully ours whilst expressing the justifiable anger we feel at having had this taken away from us so many years ago.

Jenny – a client with an Action Taker wound

At work, Jenny is seen as a bit of a bully. She has been known to shout at people when they don't meet their deadlines and she can be cold and inflexible when people ask her for time off. Others sometimes feel flattened by her strong opinions, and she doesn't listen to any of the feedback she receives. Although she has some good friends at work, other colleagues fear her anger and try to avoid having to deal with her directly.

Jenny has never been unduly upset by the reputation she has. She runs a good department that has won many awards. She believes that the way she is has contributed to this success and has ensured that things have been done efficiently and effectively. However, recently something happened that did upset Jenny very much. Her fifteen-year-old daughter moved out to live with her best friend, saying she could no longer take her mum's domineering behaviour and her fits of rage.

This shattered Jenny's world. She knew she could be aggressive, but she thought her children understood that she loved them deeply. She felt shame when she treated them badly and often apologised, hoping this would make things OK. Now she could no longer lie to herself. She felt intense shame around what had happened and knew she was in the wrong.

A colleague said he thought Jenny should get some professional support around the situation with her daughter, but Jenny responded with anger, biting her colleague's head off and telling him it was none of his business. However, later that night, once she had calmed down, Jenny talked it through with her ex-partner, who suggested a place she could go that specialised in working with anger. Jenny relented and booked in a series of sessions with Ella.

Sitting in Ella's room in the first session Jenny was furious. 'I know you're judging me. You think I'm a bully and a bad mother. I don't know why I have even come here. You look like butter wouldn't melt in your mouth; you couldn't fight your way out of a paper bag. I can't stand weak people; I need someone much stronger than you.'

Ella was a little taken aback, but she tried her best to understand and to find out more about what was going on for Jenny. 'I am not surprised you are angry. I would be angry if I thought I was judged in that way. It must be really painful for you to think others have those ideas about you. Do you often worry that people are judging you like that?'

'Yes, I know my work colleagues think I'm a bully. So does my ex-partner and my daughter. And now I come here, and I can tell you think the same.'

'Well. Seeing as you're here now, I suggest we explore this a bit further if that's OK with you? We could take a look at those judgements you feel you're receiving from me and explore them a bit more.'

Jenny agreed, and they got a whiteboard out on the carpet to represent Ella and wrote up all the messages Jenny was hearing from her:

You are a tyrant.

I am frightened of you.

I don't want to get to know you.

You're dangerous.

No wonder everyone leaves you.

They then discussed the messages and Jenny saw that they were identical to the messages she was hearing from her colleagues, friends, children and ex-partner. She chose a red cloth to put over the board to go with this set of messages. Ella then asked Jenny when she might first have heard such messages.

'I first heard things like this when I was a teenager and I was always getting into fights and bullying other girls. The teachers hated me and told me I was dangerous. I wasn't like that at home though. At home, I was terrified of my mum – she dominated us all. In fact, thinking about it, I thought all of these same messages about my mum. I used to say to my gran that she was a tyrant and I thought she was dangerous. I was sure she would kill my dad one day; they had such loud fights and my dad just couldn't stand up for himself – physically or emotionally. She never hurt him that badly, but one day I was sure she would. The one time I tried to stand up to her she pulled me upstairs by my hair and threw me into my room. When I tried to talk to my dad about the violence, he denied there was a problem. I didn't exist to them in the midst of their battles. I felt unseen and they took no notice of my protests.'

They then got another board out to represent Jenny's mum so they could explore the messages Jenny had received from her during her childhood. These were:

You have no say.

I am the boss.

Get lost.

Shut up.

If you want to stay safe keep quiet.

You have no rights in this house.

With a heavy heart Jenny saw these were the *same* messages her children had been receiving from her for all these years. Although she had never hurt them physically, her behaviour had nevertheless had a damaging effect and left them feeling scared and unsafe. She looked up and saw compassion in Ella's face. She was so grateful to see that Ella wasn't judging her for the way she had been, but was clearly feeling warmth towards her, and was by her side as she experienced this revelation.

Jenny then chose to represent her thirteen-year-old self on the carpet. She placed herself in a corner, hiding, far away from her mum. When Jenny stepped into this part of herself, she felt a mixture of fear and anger. She felt the rage she had felt as a child about her mum's violent behaviour and she also felt how terrified she had been of crossing her, and remembered how much time she had spent hiding from her.

Once she was back in her chair, the first thing Jenny wanted to do was to bring some support to this young part of herself. She could see now how impossible the situation had been for her. She had been given two role models: one who was aggressive and bullying; and one who was submissive and vulnerable. She could quite see why she had chosen to go down the route of being aggressive and bullying. Under the circumstances, being submissive and vulnerable just seemed too dangerous.

So she stepped into a loving part of herself that brought compassion and understanding to the thirteen-year-old who had been terrified of her mum and vilified by her teachers. After receiving this support, the thirteen-year-old girl found that she felt even more angry with her mum. With someone else on her side, it was clearer now how unfairly she had been treated. After discussing this for a while with Ella, Jenny decided she wanted to step back into the place of the thirteen-year-old girl and stand up to her mum and get her out of her inner world. With the supportive part by her side, she felt that she would now have the courage to stand up to her.

So Ella got a bat and a cushion and set up the piece of work safely for Jenny. She explained how to use the bat in a way that wouldn't cause her injury and that would ensure Jenny didn't damage anything in the room. Ella was aware it was really important for Jenny to have a safe experience of anger now, after having had so many unsafe and damaging experiences of anger in her childhood.

Jenny stepped back into the thirteen-year-old girl and knelt down in front of the cushion, facing her mum. She had the supportive part by her side and Ella read out the caring words this part had said. Jenny was then finally able to express all the anger she felt towards her mum, which had remained unexpressed in her for so many years. She beat the cushion as she told her how unfair it had been, how frightened she had been of her, and what a bully and a coward she thought she was. She felt very powerful as she spoke her truth and expressed her anger.

Eventually, when Jenny felt she was strong enough to overpower her mum, she summoned up all the strength she could and beat the cushion with full force, roaring at her, demanding that she leave. She commanded her mum to get out of her inner world, telling her that she was no longer willing to live with the messages she had given her. Ella slowly moved the whiteboard off the carpet as Jenny beat the cushion and ordered her mum to go away and leave her alone.

Following this process, Jenny felt exhilarated. She had never expressed her anger in this way before and she felt empowered and free. Jenny and Ella sat back in their chairs and talked for a while, surveying the new scene in front of them. Jenny's mum was now gone from the carpet, and this gave her a sense of safety, calm and ease. There seemed to be so much space now and life looked lighter and brighter to her. She could feel her whole body relax.

10.

The Transformer Archetype

Our Transformer is the part of us that gains perspective and sees things clearly. Our Transformer holds our intellectual ability and comes up with skilful strategies to keep us safe in our lives.

Qualities of the Transformer archetype in its fullness

Having perspective and seeing clearly

Our Transformer is the part of us that can step back and really see what is going on. This is the side of us that can detach from the situation, get perspective and look at things clearly and unemotionally. Our Transformer has the ability to reserve judgement and to see things from many different points of view. From this stepped-back position, they can reframe situations for us so we can see them differently, and they can generate new options for us and show us all the different possibilities available to us.

The Transformer is not attached to any particular way of seeing things or any particular outcome. This part of us is dispassionate and lacks the warmth and morality of the Heart Centred Leader. However, this lack of attachment is necessary to allow us to see things in a different light and thereby change our thinking.

Intellectual thought

Our Transformer resides in our mind and is very closely associated with left-brain thinking and processing. This side of us is intelligent, clear-headed, precise and relentless in its pursuit of detail. The Transformer relishes an intellectual challenge and leaves no stone unturned in finding ingenious solutions to problems and generating new ways forward.

Due to the Transformer's lack of morality, these gifts and what they create can be used for 'good' or 'ill'. The Transformer is equally content developing an atomic bomb, a cure for cancer, a space probe or a new theme park. Within each of us, our Transformer needs the guidance of our Heart Centred Leader if we are to channel our gifts in a way which serves our overall vision and helps us tread the path we wish to take in life.

Bringing about transformation

The role of the Transformer is, as the name suggests, to bring about transformation in our lives. The ultimate form of 'seeing things differently' is to experience a complete paradigm shift in which we see our whole life experience from a different point of view. Our thinking – and the way we live our lives – is then transformed.

In Healing The Shadow the type of healing we aim for is not simply about achieving the absence of any previous pain or struggle – it is also about bringing transformation to the way people see themselves, how they experience their lives and what is possible for them. The Transformer is the archetype that allows for this kind of new thinking, which some people might see as a shift to a higher level of awareness or some kind of spiritual or personal evolution.

Transformation can come about in seemingly mystical or magical ways. Sometimes it comes as a flash of inspiration or a sudden insight, the cause of which we cannot pinpoint. Hence a common name for this archetype has historically been the Magician. Alternatively, transformation can come about as a result of taking a series of clear, rigorous steps that produce, at the end, something that appears quite magical. The development of the internet might be a good example of this second type of transformation. Thanks to the internet we are now able to see and speak to people on the other side of the world, and to find information at the press of a button. The use of the intellect, combined with rigorous hard work and clear logical steps, has created something seemingly magical.

Generally, we believe a mixture of both of these aspects is needed to bring about transformation. We see both the 'recipe' from which the Transformer starts and the 'magical' moments the Transformer creates as going hand in hand. Sometimes inspiration comes first, leading us to a series of logical steps that need to be taken in order for transformation to occur. Other times, a series of logical, carefully executed steps is followed by moments of inspiration, insight and transformation. For example, in a Healing The Shadow process we follow a series of well-defined steps which, when appropriately used, can lead to sudden, transformational and often unexpected results.

Self-protection

Our Transformer plays a particularly crucial role in childhood, where it helps to protect us and keep us safe. The aspect of the Transformer that takes this role plays such an important part in our lives that we give it a special name – the Safety Officer.

The Safety Officer constantly scans around for danger. They need to do this, particularly in childhood, when we are small and extremely vulnerable and unable to physically or emotionally look after ourselves or stand up for ourselves effectively. The Safety Officer scans our environment for danger so that they can warn us when we need to take preventative action. They learn what kind of situations might spell danger for us, and are highly attuned to the finer nuances of these during our childhood and later in life.

Once they identify such situations, they then work out the best strategy for us to employ for our survival. The fight or flight responses of the Action Taker are not usually an option for us as children. How could a child fight the adults around them when they are so much bigger and more powerful than they are? Where would a child flee to? Children all need to rely on their Transformer archetype to come up with other options, and the part we call the Safety Officer is extremely good at this.

Such options may be:

- To go quiet

- To hide

- To be very still

- To cry

- To not cry

- To appease and please

- To 'be good'

- To 'zone out'

- To pretend to be happy

- To pretend to be sad

- To pretend to be frightened

- To excel at something

- To fail at something

- To take a particular person's side...

And a myriad other, often quite complex, strategies.

As children, we tend to employ whatever strategy the Safety Officer, from their assessment of the situation, concludes will be safest for us. There is no morality in the Safety Officer, as they struggle for our physical and emotional survival. Safety is the only goal. They may advise us to steal, to lie, to be duplicitous, to blame or frame others, and more.

The Safety Officer uses Transformer skills for working out which situations are dangerous; then they think very quickly, seeing all the options available, before generating the best possible solutions for us. They then become very attached to scanning for the particular threats they have identified and then employing the particular strategies they have devised. They will relentlessly and tirelessly work for our safety, whatever it takes. Often our Safety Officer will continue to do this for many years, even long after the original threat has diminished or disappeared.

The Safety Officer will also generate beliefs about us to keep us safe. Holding these beliefs can help us to behave in ways that are less likely to cause danger for us.

Examples might be:

- *I am a naturally quiet person*

- *I am always helpful and loving*

- *I am a naughty boy*

- *I was born with something wrong with me*

- *Everything is always my fault*

- *I'm stupid and useless*

- *I am not a likeable person*

- *I'm better than anyone else around here*

- *I am not an interesting person*

- *These people don't deserve me*

- *I'm the only one around here who can sort things out*

- *I'm responsible for everything.*

And so on, ad infinitum. They will hold tightly to these ideas, not because they are true but because believing them will help us adopt the most appropriate behaviour to maintain safety within the particular family environment in which we are being raised.

Rising up and above

We find that the element of air is a good representation of the Transformer archetype. The Transformer rises up and has perspective, as if suspended high up in the air. From here they can see clearly. We think of our mind as being able to 'take flight' in a way that the rest of our body cannot.

The 'magical' nature of the Transformer can also be represented by air imagery. Things magically 'vanish into thin air' and people fly in the air on their magic carpets.

Surviving at any cost

In the Transformer archetype the animal instinct is the instinct of survival. Here, we are talking about our immediate survival: 'It's you or it's me.'

This is typified in nature by the predator/prey dynamic. As animals, we carry within us the instinct to predate, and we also carry within us the instinctive fear of others predating on us, and the behaviours necessary to avoid this threat.

We believe humans are hardwired to be predators. We are capable of killing other living creatures in order to fulfil our own needs. Indeed, our survival, in the past at least, depended on this. We are hardwired to employ the qualities of the Transformer to predate on other creatures in this way. For example, we need to make use of our Transformer's ability to be dispassionate – we will not be able to follow through on what we need to do if we feel compassion for the creatures we hunt. We also need to use our intellect, cunning and logic to entrap our prey; this is all the territory of the Transformer. The basic premise here is, 'My survival depends on me destroying you'. There is no middle way; there is no place for negotiation – we can't both survive.

Most of us don't wish to be seen as a predator. It's a term that is generally used in a derogatory way in our society. However, we all have this instinct within us, and getting to know it will serve us better than putting it into shadow. Once we know our internal predator, we can make a conscious choice around whether or not to act from this place.

Similarly, we are hardwired as prey. We carry the instinct to look out and to scan the environment for danger. We instinctively know how to hide or to camouflage ourselves to avoid detection. It is important to get to know this part of ourselves that fears attack. That way we can gain conscious control over these defensive behaviours and come to understand when it might be appropriate to behave in these ways and when it might not serve us to do so.

Feeling fear

Fear is the emotion that opens the doorway to a healthy and vibrant connection with our Transformer. We need to have the ability to face and feel our fear, and yet not be overwhelmed or paralysed by it, if we are to have access to the insights and transformation this archetype has to offer us.

For many of us, facing our deepest fears is no small task. We either 'go for it' and face our fear, or we live in a place of denial and avoidance – there is little middle ground. This is one reason the Transformer archetype tends to see things as 'black or white'. We are either in the light or in the dark, we see or don't see, we are enlightened or ignorant, we are in heaven or in hell.

Given the traumatic fear that high numbers of us experience in our childhood, it is easy for this archetype to remain 'in the dark' for a whole lifetime. Without the necessary support and guidance, many people find that allowing themselves to finally feel and process the terror of their childhood experiences remains too daunting a task.

Being aware of our judgements and communicating these clearly

The Transformer assesses every situation and makes judgements about it. These are not 'facts' but are 'best guesses' based on our previous experiences. Our healthy adult Transformer can offer us these judgements without attachment, and can own that they are not necessarily the truth. We can then share these openly and cleanly with others.

For example, if a friend tells us that she is very busy in her life at the moment, we might make a judgement that she won't have time to meet up for our weekly Thursday night drink. We might say: 'Gemma, when you said you were very busy at work, I started to think that maybe you'd rather not go out for our usual drink on Thursday. I just thought I'd check in case you need that time free to work.'

This is open and clear communication in which we are owning our 'best guesses' as just that, and leaving the other person space to refute them or agree with them.

If our Safety Officer is still active from childhood, and is in overdrive to protect us from threats that probably no longer exist, then many of these 'best guesses' can be way off the mark.

A man looks at a woman on the bus. She may guess:

He fancies me, he might rape me.

He's looking at my expensive new bag – he's going to rob me.

He thinks I'm ugly, he's mocking me.

He thinks I'm pretty, he's going to overwhelm me with attention.

He thinks I'm stupid, he's going to shame me.

He hates me, he might hit me.

And so the list goes on. All these 'judgements' could be made by different women, based on the same look from the same man.

Our Safety Officer will not easily let such judgements go. They are very attached to protecting us, no matter what the cost may be. The more we are forewarned of possible threats, the better chance we have of taking some preventative action. Because of this attachment to protecting us, they are likely to see these judgements as 'the truth', rather than just as a 'best guess'.

So they will say things like:

I can tell you don't want to meet for a drink this week.

I just knew that man wanted to steal my wallet.

You've never respected me.

And so on. They will make judgements and speak as if their fears and fantasies are the truth and will not allow anyone else the space to refute them.

Messages that wound our Transformer

There are certain messages that particularly harm our ability to embody the Transformer archetype in a healthy way. These are messages that suggest we are bad, or wrong, or rotten at our core.

If we have received the message that we are 'bad' in this way – that we are irredeemably, fundamentally flawed – our Transformer energy will be wounded. We will fear other people seeing this 'badness' in us, and our Transformer will spend their time trying to make sure that no one else finds out 'what we're really like'. This leaves little time to perform other Transformer duties.

The terms 'bad', 'badness' and 'what we're really like' are in quotation marks because it's important to remember, when working with the Transformer archetype, that these are perceptions on the part of the individual concerned. They are beliefs taken on during childhood to protect us in some way and help us to survive. In Healing The Shadow we don't believe that anyone is totally or irredeemably bad or evil, although of course people do bad things.

There is one very common way that this 'badness' wound gets created, and it is worth explaining this in detail here. This 'badness' wound can form due to a particular reframe that the Transformer may make when a child is experiencing trauma, particularly if they are being seriously abused, be that physically, sexually or emotionally.

First, the child's Transformer steps back and looks at what's happening from a distance. They see somebody doing something bad to the child. However, that is too scary for them to take on as a reality, especially if the child is utterly dependent on the person who's being 'bad'. So their Transformer will find a way to look at the situation differently. It's very common for the Transformer to reframe what is happening by having the child conclude: 'No. That person is not bad. *I'm* bad. *I've* done something very bad and that's why this is happening to me.' This is another way of seeing the situation. It's actually not true, but the child's Transformer may choose to interpret things that way because it helps the child to feel safer.

The child feels safer because if *they* are doing something bad then they have some power in the situation: they can try to stop being bad. This shift of perception gives the child some sense of control over what's happening to them; the child is able to believe that if they can change their behaviour, then they might be able to stop the abuse from happening.

However, if the child sees what's happening as someone else just being bad towards them for no reason, then they have to see that they have *no control* over the situation at all, and this is just too terrifying. This is an example of the very clever, very contorted kind of thinking of which the Transformer is capable.

Many of us find that we've believed this kind of lie about ourselves from childhood, and we grow up believing that we're bad or dysfunctional or wrong in some way. Actually, it's just our Transformer playing a very clever trick on us – not to harm us, but to help us survive by keeping us psychologically safe.

Shadows of the wounded Transformer

If we have taken on the belief that we are bad or wrong or rotten in some way, then our Transformer will be wounded and this energy will show up in unconscious shadowy ways we don't really understand.

Inflated behaviours

In response to believing the message that we are 'bad', we may inflate our Transformer energy and become extremely adept at hiding anything we fear may be 'bad' in ourselves. We watch ourselves constantly to see if we are getting anything wrong, and we control our behaviour minutely to ensure that no 'badness' slips out.

Of course, because it is not true that we are bad (this is just a lie that we took on to help us to survive), we are in an impossible situation: trying to hide a side of ourselves that doesn't actually exist. We will never be able to relax and feel we have achieved this; we will always fear that this unidentifiable 'badness' could surprise us and sneak out at any moment if we don't remain on high alert.

This can lead to perfectionism and hypervigilance. We can be constantly 'overthinking' and trying desperately to work out what we might have done wrong and what steps we can take to avoid doing it again.

Our fear that we are bad can cause the instinctive predator part of us to go into overdrive. They desperately look for someone to destroy so that we don't get destroyed. They become a Persecutor. Our Persecutor is willing to finish off another person, and will do this with relish. They will destroy colleagues, friends, partners, even our own children, with energy and enthusiasm. This is survival: it's me or you. That dynamic makes our Persecutor a very powerful energy when it's in full force; it overtakes us, and there is no other energy that can match it. We project our feared badness onto others and then we attempt to destroy it.

At its worst, this can escalate to the most extreme forms of abuse: sexual abuse, torture, humiliation and degradation. Such a Persecutor doesn't see others as human, and appears to have lost touch with any sense of compassion or human decency.

This Persecutor energy can also act out inside our own inner world. Our Persecutor will mercilessly criticise and hate parts of us in an attempt to annihilate the 'badness' that lives inside us, once and for all. They are willing to sacrifice any aspect of us – our liveliness, our aspirations, our assertiveness, our tenderness – and they will do whatever they see as necessary in order for us not to be seen as 'bad'.

Deflated behaviours

In contrast to responding with such high-intensity reactions to the message that we are 'bad', we may, instead, deflate our Transformer side. Rather than trying to prove we're not bad, we simply hide from others to prevent being predated upon. We please and appease; we mould ourselves into whatever shape will draw the least attention. We block ourselves from *any* seeing or knowing. It is like a child hiding in the dark with their eyes closed. We become dense, fogged and unable to work anything out. We don't want to see the truth that we fear, so we hide it from ourselves. We can't see our options or make decisions. Our Transformer seems to have shut down completely, but in reality they have shut us down to try to protect us from seeing something it is too scary to see.

We may 'space out'. We may live in a make-believe alternative reality or inhabit other worlds. Others may see us as 'living on another planet' or 'dense'. Many children fail at school because their Transformer has shut them down in this way and they are unable to process information. They are not 'thick', but simply shut down as a response to deep trauma of some kind.

People with deflated Transformer energy will not persecute others, but they will relentlessly persecute themselves, feeling endless guilt and shame and unable to get any respite from their inner tormentor.

Messages that heal our Transformer

The messages we need to hear in order to heal wounded Transformer energy are:

You are innocent.

You've done nothing wrong.

You were born good, but people have lied to you and told you that you're bad.

You're still good at your core and always have been, even if you've done some bad things.

Receiving these messages can be deeply healing and can calm a troubled mind and bring peace. Since the Transformer is the archetype of the intellect, then hearing these messages verbally or receiving them in written form is extremely effective, whether this is from our friends, family, partner or therapist.

Healing processes for the Transformer

Safety Officer work

The Safety Officer is an aspect of us, described above, that develops in childhood in order to protect us, both physically and psychologically. Safety Officers are *extremely* dedicated to the job they do – of course they are, our very lives have depended on them. If they see the slightest sign of danger, they are on high alert. They immediately, fully and without question, employ the successful strategies they have developed to keep us safe and which served us so well when we were children.

Unfortunately, in adulthood, rather than recognising the important role these parts have played for us, we often feel negatively about these sides of ourselves. We resent them and see them as obstacles or blocks that are getting in the way of us living our lives. Our Safety Officers can be very sad about the way we see them, as they only want to serve us and they know how vital their role has been. But they are dedicated to keeping us safe, so they keep on doing what they believe they need to do, despite our opposition and lack of appreciation for them.

In Healing The Shadow we work with Safety Officers by listening carefully and respectfully to them and really coming to understand the important role they have played. We listen with awe and admiration as they describe the skill they have employed and the ingenuity they have used to protect the client and keep them safe. We honour them deeply for keeping the client alive and thank them for the vital role they have played. This is often a very emotional moment for the Safety Officer, as they have never before been recognised or valued – they have simply soldiered on, for years, with no thanks or appreciation.

Once the Safety Officer has been recognised and thanked for their service, they are usually open to a discussion about their role in the client's life going forward. They are often uncomfortably aware that the client is unhappy with their strategies, and they also feel exhausted from all the hard work they have been doing for so long, so they are open to new ideas. Once they are updated with new information about the current situation and the level of threat, they can then make decisions that will best serve the client in their adult life.

We often facilitate a conversation between an adult, Heart Centred Leader part of the client and their Safety Officer, so that they can discuss the role of the Safety Officer and negotiate a new way forward where they can work together in the client's best interests. The Safety Officer is usually delighted to finally gain the attention, respect and gratitude of this Heart Centred Leader part and to have the opportunity to find better ways of serving them. Their only desire all these years has been to serve the client's best interests. This is why they worked so hard to protect them all those years ago: so that they could safely emerge into adulthood and live a full, rich and rewarding life.

Persecutor work

We know that the Transformer wound is a belief that we are bad at our core. This means we grow up with the sense that there is something inside us that is wrong, broken, dangerous, repulsive or utterly abhorrent in some way, and there is no possibility of putting this right. We are tarnished, damaged goods, not human. This is a powerful and painful belief to bear. When we carry this wound, we think there is no point in trying to heal ourselves from this badness, because we see it as our true nature. So all we can do is try to hide our badness from others and make sure that we don't show our real self – we wear masks, and try to pretend we are something we are not. We put on a show that we are a 'nice' or 'good' person, whilst deep down believing we are irredeemably bad.

This belief is very frightening and deeply disconnecting. It disconnects us from others and from ourselves. We feel utterly alone, and fear rules our lives. We start to believe certain parts of us may be at the root of this 'badness' and that they could be dangerous in some way and cause harm to others. So we hide these parts away and never admit them to anyone. We are caught in a trap of isolation: we cannot possibly share these 'bad' sides of ourselves with others, as they are utterly unacceptable. We also believe we cannot change, so it would be futile to speak to anyone about these sides of ourselves.

Meanwhile these 'unacceptable' parts of us are being pushed further and further into shadow, and because we are denying them and hating and shaming them, we are becoming more and more disconnected from ourselves, as well as from others. This is particularly true when we have parts of us that want to destroy or annihilate. Parts that are utterly cruel and hateful towards us or others. We never want to show these parts to anyone for fear of being cast out and hated or being labelled as inhuman or evil.

We have a special name for these destructive parts of us, which was mentioned earlier. We call them Persecutor parts. These parts of us are never shown the light of day, and therefore they never have an opportunity to heal. They seem destined to live forever in our shadow. However, there is a way out of this trap. In

Healing The Shadow we have a process where Persecutor parts can be allowed out in the safety of the therapeutic space. This initially appears quite counterintuitive. The client is given the opportunity to step fully into this side of themselves, deliberately and consciously, and to allow it to be as destructive and cruel as it wants. They do this in the safety of a well-held therapeutic space, where there will be no real-world consequences and they cannot hurt or upset anyone in their lives.

The best way to carry out this process is with a disposable doll that the client can tear up or treat in any way they wish in order to release this energy from their body. The process is safely held and managed so that the client can allow that part to do whatever it wants to do, without causing any damage or harm to themselves or their practitioner.

Remember that shadow parts of us can only cause real harm when they come out unconsciously. They burst out in damaging ways because we have kept them hidden for so long. It is like trying to keep a beach ball under water. It takes a lot of energy to hold the ball under the water, and it takes a lot of concentration to keep it under control as it tries to escape from us. When it finally does come bursting out, it forces its way to the surface with a lot of energy. Yet once it is free and bobbing around on the surface, it is just a beach ball, full of air, that can't cause harm to anyone.

The same is true for these Persecutor parts of us. Because we are trying to hide them away so strongly, the chances are they *will* cause harm if they just burst out in an uncontrolled way in our lives. We don't know these parts of ourselves, we can't control them, and they can force their way out with a lot of power in extremely destructive ways.

So in this process, when we consciously and deliberately step into a Persecutor side of ourselves, we have already created a shift. That part no longer has the power to catch us by surprise. We are taking back control by choosing to act it out deliberately. Once the part has acted out and expended all its energy, the power is gone. It is like taking the cork out of a bottle.

However destructively these parts of us may act out, at their core this is not their true purpose, and once they have been released and allowed to express themselves in a safe space, we can start a dialogue with them and find out what they really want. In Healing The Shadow we believe that however cruel and destructive a part may seem to be, its original intention was always to serve us in some way.

After undertaking this process, people tend to feel less scared of these sides of themselves. They may still not like certain qualities of that part of themselves, but it no longer feels so dark and dangerous to them, and they feel like a safer person – for themselves and others. What's more, they can now start to claim the gold this part has to offer. These Persecutor parts can carry great gifts: power, clarity, wisdom and insight. Once we get to know these parts, they can be used as powerful allies and a force for good in our lives.

Lucy – a client with a Transformer wound

Lucy feels quite trapped in her life. At home she feels controlled and ill at ease. Her partner is highly critical and often puts her down in front of other people when they visit. Her art studio is her only sanctuary.

People tend to see Lucy as easy prey: someone they can use and abuse as they wish. Despite never openly complaining about this, she feels a lot of resentment about how others treat her and the lack of respect they show her.

Lucy shows a lot of talent for art and has tried to make a living from it, but so far she has not managed to bring in much money. She remains financially dependent on her partner, which increases her sense of vulnerability in the relationship.

Having produced some new pieces of work over the last year, Lucy is trying to establish herself in a nearby art gallery, but she is having a very difficult time with the man who runs it. This man has a history of treating younger female artists with a lack of respect, expecting them to dance to his tune if they want to have their work displayed. Lucy doesn't feel safe around him and is frightened to approach him to present her work. She has been having nightmares around the thought of contacting him, and the fear she is feeling is stopping her moving forward with what could be a very positive step for her career.

After a night of particularly disturbing nightmares, Lucy realised there was something unusual going on and that her reaction to this situation was out of proportion. She decided to get some support, and she contacted Jerry to book some sessions.

With Jerry supporting her, she explored her situation and her reactions to the gallery owner, Paul. They talked about Lucy's childhood, and she explained to Jerry that when she was six her mother's sister had died, and her cousin, James, had come to live in her home. From that time on, her life was a misery. James totally overpowered her and dominated her world. He would take up all the space in the house. He would cut the heads off her dolls and hide things he knew were of value to her. He teased and taunted her and mocked her in front of her friends. As she got older, he found out she was self-harming. He used this information against her, forcing her to run errands for him. She felt she had to do everything he asked, for fear that he would tell her mum about the self-harm. She was terrified of her parents finding out.

Lucy had already spent many years in psychotherapy, and she understood that her reaction to Paul could be linked to the experiences with her cousin. She had spoken a lot about her cousin with her previous therapists, and she shared with Jerry everything she had come to understand about the impact that this period had on her, and the anger and impotence she felt as a result.

Lucy decided to start the session by getting the gallery owner, Paul, represented on the carpet. She wanted to gain more insight into the messages she was picking up from him and why she was having such an extreme response. Jerry helped her to represent Paul on the carpet. Lucy placed the board at the far end of the carpet and chose a black cloth to drape over it. With Jerry's help she reflected on the messages she was picking up from Paul, and he wrote these up on the whiteboard:

I have all the power.

You are nothing to me.

You can't get away from me.

I can do what I want with you.

I can control your life.

I can ruin you.

Lucy felt a lot of fear as she saw Paul represented on the carpet. When they discussed the messages further, she was not surprised to find they were similar to the messages she had received from her cousin. This made a lot of sense. Her fear of

Paul in the last few weeks had been so overwhelming that it was helpful to gain a better understanding of why she was reacting so strongly. She could now see clearly that this situation wasn't only about Paul, but it was also stirring trauma from her past and evoking the same fear in her that she had felt during the years when her cousin James was living in her home.

Although it wasn't a new insight for Lucy to see that these messages were echoes of messages from her time living with James, she *was* surprised by what unfolded next. As she continued to discuss the messages on the board with Jerry, she began to see that she *herself* had a part of her that thought these things towards others. She never said them or acted them out, but with certain friends she felt she had all the power and that they were nothing to her. She felt she had the power to control them, and she could feel the part of her that might enjoy getting them to do whatever she wanted them to. This was a revelation to Lucy. Although this part of her felt in some ways strangely familiar, she had never seen it before, and she would never have admitted to anyone that she had these thoughts and feelings. Yet here in this session with Jerry, it was clear to her that she had a part like this living in her and there was no point in denying it.

They talked for a while about how to proceed with the session. Jerry explained to Lucy that some of her power may be tied up in this part of her that she had never expressed. It was clearly a very powerful part, yet she spent her time keeping it hidden, so all the power and energy it held remained locked away. He explained that, although it sounded counterintuitive, there may be some value in her stepping into that side of herself and getting to know it. She may then be able to release some of the power held there and use it to help her to move forward in her life.

Lucy was intrigued by this idea and, although she felt some fear at the thought of inhabiting that part of herself and allowing Jerry to see her acting and speaking in this way, she decided to go ahead. Jerry got out a small disposable doll and placed it on the floor. Lucy took the black cloth she had used to represent the gallery owner, Paul, and she wrapped it around herself. She began to take on his energy, the energy that she now realised also lived inside her. She looked at the little doll on the carpet and told it how powerful she was: 'I control you; you can't get away from me. I have all the power here.' She began to walk around the doll in circles, taunting it with her threats and cruel words.

After a while she told Jerry that she was feeling a little self-conscious, as she would never normally behave like this, especially not when someone else was watching her. He said he understood, and encouraged her by suggesting that she could even allow herself to *enjoy* playing this part, since no one was going to get hurt and it was a good opportunity to explore this energy in her. When she heard this, Lucy pulled herself up taller and looked down her nose at the doll. 'I have all the power,' she said again. 'I can do whatever I like to you, and you can't stop me. I am the one in charge here. I am all-powerful. I can do what I want to you, and you *will* do what I say. I can take up all the space and you just have to suffer down there. The bigger I get the smaller you get, and I love it!' Lucy then stood on the doll, carelessly, as if by accident. 'Oh, sorry!' she exclaimed. 'Did I *hurt* you? Oh whoops, there, I've done it again.' In this way she continued to toy with the doll and to feel into this place of total power.

Once Lucy had completed her ill treatment of the doll, Jerry asked her how she felt. 'I feel tall and powerful,' she said. 'As if nothing can hurt me and I can do anything I want.' Jerry asked her what she wanted to do with all this power. 'I want to be free. I want to create. I want to live and express myself.' Lucy made expansive movements with her hands as she said this and took up all the space in the room as she strode around and around.

Eventually, Jerry invited her back to her seat. She put the black cloth back over the messages from the gallery owner and came back to sit down in her chair. She was glowing with confidence and strength, and was clearly energised by the exploration. They discussed the new power she had discovered in her, and how this could be used for good in her life.

Finally, Jerry invited Lucy to look again at the carpet and the black cloth with the messages from Paul. He asked her what it was like now to see the representation of Paul on her carpet. Lucy looked at the board and the black cloth. She read through the messages. 'It's just words,' she said. 'It's just a black cloth and a few words. I still don't like the guy, but I don't feel the fear that I felt at the start of the session. That is gone. He's a bit full of himself, and has some strange ideas about how to run a gallery, but I can see that I don't need to be scared of him. He's just who he is.'

Part Three

11.

Relationship Between Client and Practitioner

The relationship between client and practitioner is key to all the work we do in Healing The Shadow. The relationship with the client holds and contains everything we will do together, and this relationship is, in itself, a part of the client's healing process. In this chapter I explain what we believe are the most important components of the client–practitioner relationship.

In Healing The Shadow we see our clients as our equals, as fellow travellers on the journey of life, and we see ourselves as having tools and techniques that can help and support our clients on this journey, along with having the capacity to hold our clients wherever their journey may take them.

We openly share our therapeutic approach with our clients and explain the ideas and beliefs we hold, along with the tools we use. This allows clients to be completely engaged in their own healing. They choose what they want to have happen at each step in each session, and we support them and facilitate them in this. We are 'being with' not 'doing to'. We stand alongside our clients as they take the journey they choose to take. Our attitude is beautifully expressed in the famous words of Ram Dass, a spiritual leader from the 1970s, who said, 'We are all just walking each other home.'[6]

Contracting

I'd like to start with what may seem like a small example: before beginning our work with a client, we don't send out a contract setting out our terms for the client to sign. We don't see our arrangement to work with a client as a legal agreement – we are not likely to take our client to court if they fail to pay for a session. This is living in an old, outdated paradigm, where those in authority 'lay down the law' in an inflexible and non-relational way. The truth is that most therapeutic clients never read the documents they are asked to sign, and therefore if an issue arises with the practitioner, the signed document is of little value and the two of them find they are starting at square one when trying to resolve the difficulty, with no solid ground between them to build on.

In Healing The Shadow we see our working relationship as a collaboration between two individuals. This relationship is at the heart of the therapeutic alliance, so it is best to start as we mean to go on, and to meet the client as a fellow human being and treat them in a respectful, transparent and human way.

We make practical agreements based on mutual respect and accommodating the client's needs as well as our own. Making agreements is a process that takes place through discussion and explanation and conversation. This means that the client is fully invested in what has been agreed. This is a far richer process than the one-sided issuing of a contract. Each interaction builds trust and strengthens the relationship. We then start our work together with a solid foundation, and this sets the tone for a mature adult-to-adult relationship going forward.

What we mean by an adult-to-adult relationship is that we are neither looking down on the client as being incapable of making clear arrangements with us and holding to boundaries, nor are we imposing on the client in a one-sided, authoritarian way. Both of these attitudes come from an outdated model of working which stems from a doctor–patient-type relationship between client and practitioner where the 'patient' is 'sick' and the doctor knows what is best for them and has the knowledge and power to 'heal' them. Such attitudes also stem from a legalistic and fear-based way of relating to others. Neither are appropriate for building a trusting relationship with a client.

As Healing The Shadow practitioners, we trust that our client has a 'grown-up' part of them that is capable of managing the world and relationships in an adult way. We trust in this even if the client is presenting in a scattered or immature manner. This trust is one of the biggest gifts we give our clients, and it is based on one of the key principles of shadow work: that we all have within us full capacity in all areas of our lives. Even though some parts of us have been put into shadow and we struggle to access them, deep down we know those parts are there. Deep down we know our wholeness and our full capacity.

If our therapist treats us as if we are incapable of managing life, part of us may be grateful for being rescued and cared for; however, another part of us will receive the message that the therapist doesn't see the whole of us and that they perceive us as limited and stuck. The part of us that holds the truth of our wholeness will experience the therapist's attitude as disrespectful, and we may feel anger towards them or lose trust in their ability to support us and help us to grow. Alternatively, being treated in this way, however kindly intended, may reinforce our belief that we are incapable of managing our lives and relationships, and we will remain stuck in an infantilised part of ourselves.

So from before we have even met our client we are building our relationship with them. We are sending them the message that we believe they have a competent adult part inside them that can make arrangements with us and interact with us in an adult way. We are demonstrating our respect for them as fellow human beings on this planet who are ultimately on the same journey as us – towards healing and wholeness.

Establishing that we know the client has a capable adult part of them is an important foundation for the work we do. As described earlier in the book, our work is based on the idea that the client has *many* different parts, and once the client is with us in a session then sides other than their mature adult will be explored and expressed, and will be held and nurtured and met appropriately. The client will immerse themselves deeply in their work and will not be in an adult state all the time during their session.

When the client enters into this vulnerable space, it is important for them to know that we respect them as a whole person and that we see their competencies and strengths. This makes it possible for them to explore vulnerable places whilst knowing and understanding that this is not the whole of them. Then in between sessions, and regarding the business end of our relationship, we send the message to the client that, alongside all the parts of themselves they explore in our sessions together, we know that they also have a competent, capable adult part. This is deeply respectful, and is fundamental to the way we hold our clients and relate to them throughout our work together.

Of course, there are times for some people when it might not be the case that they have access to the adult parts of themselves – someone in the grip of psychosis or a powerful, destructive addiction may be temporarily unable to access this place. In such instances our approach probably isn't right for them at this moment in their life, and a different form of therapy would be more suitable. It is only safe to explore shadow sides of ourselves if we have a secure adult place we can return to.

We form *real* relationships with our clients, where they matter to us and we matter to them. We see the healing relationship we form with our clients to be just as significant as the healing work they do on the carpet. These are two separate strands to the work that we do: the process work on the carpet and the relationship with the practitioner that holds this process work. We find this is a powerful combination where deep healing is possible. It is hard to heal only in relationship, and it is also hard to heal purely by doing our inner work. Yet when the two come together, magic happens.

Shame is a key driver in creating and maintaining shadow parts of us. The only way this shame is lifted is with the loving presence of another who can witness these sides of us without blame or judgement, and who can demonstrate their care and acceptance of *all* of us, including our shadow sides.

Before the first session

Our relationship with the client actually starts even before they get in touch with us. We share with prospective clients a clear description of the theoretical framework we use so that they can make their own decision as to whether or not our ideas and beliefs fit with theirs. We have videos explaining our beliefs about the shadow and the archetypes and describing what the work looks like and the different processes we use. We have footage of a live session that people can watch, to get a sense of whether or not this is right for them.

This allows the client to make a conscious choice as to whether or not this is the path they want to choose. It sends the message that their healing is in *their* hands. We trust in their capacity to choose the right modality for themselves. We trust in their ability to understand the concepts and ideas we work with and to see how these could apply to their own healing and growth. It means that before we start the first session, we are on the same page as our clients around their healing process. We have a common language. They meet us as adults, interested in and engaged with their own healing. We meet them as adults, committed to being with them on their journey and to bringing all our care and skill to facilitating them effectively and to meeting them with our full humanity.

There is another important step in our relationship with the client that we take before we meet them. Once our clients are booked in for their first session, we send them a detailed confidential form to complete, where they can share anything they wish to with us about their lives to date. This starts the work with an air of transparency and sends a message to our clients that whatever happened to them in their past, whatever issues they want to bring, they are welcome, and we are willing to go there and explore that territory if that is what they want to do. We ask questions about things that the client may fear aren't welcome or that they might worry it is not safe to talk about, such as physical and sexual abuse, suicidal thoughts, trauma, abandonment and neglect. The client can write as much or as little as they wish.

In asking these questions we send the message that it is possible for these subjects to be spoken about and that we have the capacity and willingness to go into this territory with the client, whilst also, of course, not requiring them to explore or talk about anything they don't wish to share. We are talking to the part of the client that wants to bring these topics out of the shadow, and we are sending the clear message: 'This is possible here. You don't have to worry about the intensity or depth of anything you bring.' This message is vital to therapeutic work, as so many people believe that certain things are not to be talked about – that they are the only one who has had that experience or thought, or that people don't want to know, or don't have the capacity to hold the subject matter. So a message that such topics are expected and welcome is refreshing, and brings relief to many people.

We find this approach works exceptionally well and is very permission-giving. After filling in the form, people arrive feeling confident and ready to talk about what they *really* want to explore in the session, whilst also knowing that the choice is absolutely theirs and they are in control of what they do and the pace at which the work unfolds. It is an essential aspect of this work that clients know they are welcome to set their boundaries and not to work on anything they don't wish to work on, and that the part of them that wants to keep certain things hidden and unspoken is welcome without question.

The client leads the session

So once we are finally with the client, after spending time welcoming them and connecting with them, the first step is to find out what they are wanting from the session. As mentioned in Chapter 1, we call this the Guiding Want. Again, we are engaging with the client's adult, the part that wants the best for them and has a vision about their life and their healing and growth. We are inviting them to take charge of their process from the start. As the client talks about what is going on for them, it may take an hour or more for them to settle clearly on what is most important for them and the shift they would like to see for themselves in that session. It can take time for the client to settle from the business and demands of everyday life and to get clarity on what is *really* going on for them and what they *really* want.

Inviting someone to answer the question of what they are wanting for themselves from a session is a whole piece of therapeutic work in itself, not least because this requires them to be able to imagine what they are wanting, just a little bit, in order for them to name and describe it. So already a shift is happening in them as they picture this. Once the Guiding Want is decided upon, the client often brightens. There is excitement and also relaxation; an important truth has been spoken, and the journey begins.

As we get started with the work, we will, more often than not, meet parts of the client that *don't* want to explore or resolve this issue. This is natural, and we spend a great deal of time working with parts that see risks for the client and don't want the work to go ahead. This is an essential part of the work we do. So whilst a client might want to work on a particular topic, we may spend a long time in the first part of the session working with the parts of them that don't want to explore this subject. In fact, hearing and exploring these parts can often be where the deeper work lies, and can be of greater value to the client than working on the topic itself.

However the work unfolds, the client has complete control over the session. They will decide at each step which part of themselves they wish to step into and explore, or what external person they wish to bring onto the carpet. This is hugely empowering for the client and forms a collaborative way of working where the client and the practitioner are working *together* to explore something. The practitioner isn't needing in any way to second-guess what the client needs or what might be best for them.

Once all parts have been fully embodied and explored and laid out on the carpet, the client chooses the shift they would like to see in their inner world. The practitioner then supports them in stepping back onto the carpet to bring about this shift for themselves. The practitioner will explain clearly what the chosen process entails, and they will discuss it fully with the client so that they understand what they are going to do and how they are going to do it, and so that they are sure that it is aligned with the shift they are looking for.

Having completed the process work, the client will be asked how they want to end the session. This allows them to be in charge of the closing moments. They are aware the end of the session is coming and can choose a gracious way to end that leaves them feeling the work is closed for that day.

Challenge and growth

Most therapists aim to work with unconditional positive regard; however, there can be a difficulty in this, as it can result in a lack of healthy challenge for the client around where their wounds are and where they need to grow. The therapist, despite their best intentions of positive regard, can be left with judgements and frustrations around the client that are left unexpressed. This is not conducive to a healthy, open, respectful and transparent relationship.

The way that we work in the room, sitting the client and practitioner side by side, with the client's inner world represented on the carpet in front of them, allows the client and practitioner to reflect on what is happening on the carpet and to discuss this together. As practitioner and client are both watching the picture unfold in front of them, the client can see as clearly as the practitioner can what the dynamics in their life are, where the shadows are and what is necessary for their growth and healing. The practitioner is never in a place of having to point anything out or to help the client see anything. They are genuinely working alongside each other, unravelling the puzzle that is laid out in front of them and allowing the client to draw their own conclusions, have their own insights and choose the process they believe will be best for them.

This makes it possible for the practitioner to *genuinely* welcome the client exactly as they are, without an agenda or judgements about how they need to change or what would be best for them. The practitioner can trust that the client will see what they need to see and have their own insights and choose their own path.

We find, because of the way Healing The Shadow work unfolds, that the client challenges *themselves* during their sessions, relieving the practitioner of any need to intervene or to express any judgements they may be forming. Once the client sees one part laid out on the carpet, we then explore the client's reaction to that part. At this point they may express judgements, frustration, lack of acceptance, opposing opinions and so on, just as Joe expressed dislike of the blue part of himself when Sam read out the words that part had spoken.

We find that it is important to give the client the opportunity to reflect on what they see on the carpet and to express any negative judgements they might have. Negative judgements are a crucial aspect of working with the shadow. If these negative judgements are not shared by the client, the practitioner can find they are left 'holding' these judgements themselves. It is as if, when these are *not* being expressed by the client, they try to find expression elsewhere, and end up landing with the practitioner, who finds themselves holding these judgements that the client hasn't spoken. This is the nature of the shadow: if it is not owned by us, it will show up externally in other ways in our world. In this instance what is not owned by the client is showing up in the practitioner instead. This is a process similar to the processes of projection and transference described in Chapter 4.

It can be very uncomfortable for a practitioner when they find themselves having judgemental thoughts about the client they are meant to be supporting unconditionally. As Healing The Shadow practitioners we understand this process and are not therefore unduly perturbed if we find ourselves having judgemental thoughts about our clients. We know we will be able to come back into a place of unconditional positive regard once this judgement has been expressed by the client themselves, and the way the sessions are set up allows ample opportunity for the client to see and express these judgements to us. These reactions that the client has expressed can then be represented as a part on the carpet and the conflict is now clearly represented as being inside the client, not between client and practitioner. The practitioner can then simply support the client in resolving this conflict, rather than finding they are taking up a position in opposition to any part of the client.

So as we learn to work with this mixture of thoughts and feelings that are in the space, we recognise that as practitioners we can pick up on unexpressed parts of the client and temporarily feel these as our own. This means that, in the same way as we pick up on judgements and harsh reactions which belong to the client, we also find we pick up on great insights and ways forward which actually originate in the client. We may find we have had a great idea for a way forward, but we hold back, understanding this is likely to belong to the client rather than to us. We believe it is not our job to express these insights or ways forward, and we try never to interpret or suggest solutions. Rather, we create a space where the client can discover these answers that already live within them.

After we have had a brilliant insight or idea, we often find, having held back from expressing it ourselves, that the client will suggest the exact same thing. This is a much more empowering way of working for the client, as they get a sense of their own capacity. When we make suggestions ourselves, we can leave the client with a sense of reliance on us, and the belief we have some kind of gift or knowledge that they don't have.

So part of our stance as practitioners is holding a belief that the client has the answers within themselves. This again comes back to trusting that they have all parts somewhere in them, even if they are not presenting themselves openly to us in that moment. It is our role to support the client in finding these wise parts of themselves, rather than to get caught up in thinking we know the answers or the right way forward. This is an act of faith, which is eventually borne out by experience when, as practitioners, time after time we witness our clients finding clever and unexpected solutions for themselves that we would never have imagined or suggested. This process is awe-inspiring to witness.

Seeing gold in our clients

Our attitude to our clients is that they have greatness and magnificence in them, and we draw on this whenever possible and encourage these sides of them to be expressed. We don't stop at holding the hope for healing the trauma or difficulty the client is experiencing – we also hold the hope for a complete transformation of their lives so that they can begin to live and love in ways they would never previously have believed possible, and to be fulfilled in their life, their work and their relationships.

This again is a manifestation of our belief that we are all equal on this journey through life. We don't limit our ideas of our clients because they carry trauma or wounding or because they are struggling in their lives; we want and hope for the absolute best for them. We know from our own experience that transformation is possible and that we ourselves have prevailed in the face of the overwhelming impact of our own wounds and the trauma we carry. We want this for our clients too, and for them to live the lives they long to live and to fulfil their wildest dreams.

This attitude in itself is deeply healing for the client. To have someone championing their success and their growth and believing that this is possible for them, to have their strengths and their gifts celebrated, to have someone seeing them in their most wounded places whilst *also* bearing witness to their greatness and celebrating their success can be life-changing.

Most of us won't be fully healed in this lifetime (whatever we may believe 'healed' would look like). But we can nevertheless live rich and full lives and offer our gifts to the world. We know this first-hand as practitioners – we have been on this journey ourselves and offer our gifts to the world whilst continuing to work on our own wounds and traumas. We understand that our wounds are our gifts and that this is true for our clients also.

This attitude of respect towards the client comes from practitioners having worked on themselves deeply and having witnessed their colleagues work there also. So the practitioner has been seen and known and accepted and loved for their strengths as well as their wounds. They have been accepted and loved in both places. They have experienced the same healing attitude that they now offer to their clients.

We recognise the strength it takes for the client to inhabit and explore the deep places they go to. We understand the paradox that the ability to explore small, frightened, vulnerable and shameful places is, in itself, a huge strength. We recognise the enormous amount of work the client has already done on themselves to get to where they are now in their life, before they even meet us.

We hold a conscious awareness not to define or limit our clients. We recognise that people can be brilliantly gifted and deeply flawed. People can grow and flourish as they heal, carrying their wounds with them in as dignified a way as possible. This work is about becoming whole rather than becoming perfect. It's about becoming more of who we really are.

We send the message to our clients that they don't have to be healed or perfect to live a full and rich life. They can start now. They just need to know themselves as well as they can and make their best decisions from there. In Healing The Shadow we understand there is no 'good' and no 'bad'. *All* parts of us are to be honoured and are serving us in some way. There is gold in every shadow and there is shadow in every golden aspect. Our so-called dysfunctions can point the way towards meeting our deepest longings and they contain the seeds of our soul's purpose in life.

Knowing ourselves and our shadows

Because the relationship with the practitioner is so important, the maturity of the practitioner is considered key in our work in Healing The Shadow. Our practitioners need to know themselves and their own shadows so that they can continue to maintain a supportive adult relationship with their client and not allow their own shadows and wounds to obscure or block the process or to unwittingly diminish or shame the client.

We work constantly with our trainees around their reactions to their client in each moment – not so that they can use this reaction to teach or 'help' the client but so that they can work with this reaction themselves in order to regain their mature, supportive, adult place in relation to the client and to be fully present and open to them. Therapeutic work can so easily be blocked by a practitioner's unconscious reactions, such as their avoidance of exploring a particular topic or their unwillingness to accept certain aspects of the client.

We work with the practitioner's reactions and support them in accepting and holding these within themselves. Once made conscious and accepted within the practitioner, such reactions can deepen their understanding of the client, and can be used to serve the client rather than creating a barrier to the work.

In the same way that we welcome all parts of the client into the room and believe they are all of value, we also welcome all parts of the practitioner into the room and believe these, too, are all of value. So rather than requiring the practitioner to maintain a position of unconditional positive regard by denying and hiding away 'unhelpful' sides of themselves, we invite them to accept such parts and to know they are not 'wrong' or 'bad' for having such reactions. They can then explore these parts and enquire as to the wisdom these parts may be bringing, whether this is insights into themselves or information that could serve them as they work with the client in their session. This is an internal process, which our trainees become skilled at carrying out alongside their facilitation of the client's process. After this exploration, the practitioner can naturally bring themselves back into a mature and supportive adult relationship with the client. This is part of what we call the Enfoldment Principle. We treat ourselves, as practitioners, in the same way as we treat our clients. We are not outside of that healing loop. So we accept all parts of ourselves in each moment, in the same way that we accept all parts of the client in each moment.

This acceptance of ourselves includes working with our reaction to our client's power, excellence, magnificence or success. Powerful parts of the client can be intimidating for the practitioner, especially when the client is going beyond where the practitioner has gone in their own life. It requires maturity and self-love to encourage and celebrate a client in going further in a particular area of their life than you yourself have been.

Building relationships with disowned parts of the client

Fundamental to the work we do is the attitude we hold towards blocks, resistance, obstacles, laziness, apathy, jealousy, vindictiveness and any other apparent 'barriers' to the client's healing. I have already talked about the deep respect we hold for all parts of the client, and this very much applies to these parts that the client themselves doesn't want to have and that we could easily be drawn into believing are a nuisance or an embarrassment and needing to be eradicated.

We work closely with these parts and spend much time speaking with them and finding out what they think and feel, what their role is and what they are trying to achieve. Our work is to form a loving connection with these parts. We give them all our time and attention and treat them with reverence, respect and care. We understand the pain they are carrying and the important role they are playing. We don't stop exploring until we have found value in them, even if the parts themselves don't believe they have any value.

This is some of the most transformational work we do. Parts that have been banished, ignored or hated for many years come back into the light and are accepted and welcomed, first by the practitioner and then by the client. As they come to more deeply understand these sides of themselves and find gratitude for what these parts have done for them throughout their life, the client develops ways to work in harmony with these parts rather than against them.

So as practitioners we work in harmony with all parts of our client at all times – whichever parts are being explored and expressed – knowing they deserve deep respect and are there to serve the client and their process.

Teaching theory

There is one final aspect to our work which is also worth mentioning here: our role in sharing theoretical ideas and beliefs with the client.

When we believe it could be helpful to our clients, we see it as our place to offer some theory that may be relevant to them. Contrary to analysing our clients or interpreting their situation or offering solutions, all of which we avoid doing, we believe we do have a role to play in sharing our theoretical framework when it could be helpful for the client. This is a very different type of interaction. It is an adult-to-adult interaction rather than a 'doctor–patient' interaction where we are analysing or interpreting.

If we notice a certain piece of theory that could relate to our client and their circumstances, we will explain to them clearly why we have arrived at the idea that this theory might be helpful, based on what they have been telling us. If they are interested, we will then share our knowledge with them. We won't bring any further interpretation of how this might relate to them; instead we will ask them how this information lands with them and what their thoughts are.

So, for example, if a client has talked about often feeling sad, believing they are needy or unwanted and struggling with addictions, then we might want to share some information about the Feeling Body archetype with them so they have a framework that could help them to make more sense of what is going on for them. We would explain that they have talked about sadness, addiction and feeling needy and unwanted, and that in our framework all these things are related to the Feeling Body archetype. They will already have heard about this in the videos they watched before the session, so it will not be a completely new idea to them.

We might ask them how they feel about the Feeling Body archetype and if they'd like us to explain a bit more about how we understand it. With permission, we may then describe what we see as the pathways to healing. Such teaching is done sparingly and with the consent of the client. We believe it is an essential part of holding a transparent adult-to-adult relationship that if we have some theory we feel may be helpful for the client, we share it with them rather than keeping it to ourselves. They are then able to decide whether or not what we are describing lands with them and if it is something they'd like to explore further. Many clients find our theoretical framework incredibly helpful in giving them a map and a way to understand themselves and their healing journey.

Using clean language

You can hopefully see, from the care we take when we introduce theory into our sessions, that we work hard to be as transparent and 'clean' with our clients as possible. By 'clean' we mean that we aim not to interpret or lead in any way and not to hold any agenda of our own. Aside from sharing theory with the client, we don't bring in any of our own opinions, thoughts or ideas. In service to this we use a certain style of questions that were developed by the psychotherapist David Grove in the 1980s. His questions, known as 'clean language', were designed to support therapists in keeping their own thoughts and assumptions out of conversations as much as possible.[7]

So our practitioners use clean language to ensure they don't bring their own influences to bear on the process. Yet not bringing our own opinions or agendas doesn't mean we are not deeply engaged in the process – quite the opposite. Paradoxically, the more we can ensure our own ideas and beliefs are put to one side, the more we can be fully present with our client. This is one of the many paradoxes we work with in Healing The Shadow. The more clean and open the practitioner is in their interactions, and the more they keep their own thoughts and ideas out of the session, the more deeply they can connect with the client and the more they can bring their full selves to the process.

12.

A Trauma-centric Practice

Hasani stares at the carpet in front of him, just about managing to keep his tears at bay. 'I thought I had a happy childhood,' he says as he surveys the scene. He stares, dazed, at the devastating messages he received from his parents, alongside the parts of him represented on the carpet that were so frightened, angry and sad when he was a child. 'My parents did the best they could for me, and I never went without anything. I've always thought it would be insulting to people who had experienced *real* trauma if I claimed that what happened to me was traumatic. I thought it was just normal childhood stuff. I've always told myself not to complain, and to be strong, and to face things like a man. But inside I always feel so weak.'

Hasani has experienced severe depression for most of his adult life, and after ten years of struggle and some recent distressing situations with his partner, he has come to seek support from a Healing The Shadow practitioner.

Hasani is not alone. The denial of childhood difficulties is common amongst people experiencing emotional challenges. In fact, believing nothing bad happened to us can often be part and parcel of the whole trauma experience. One of the most damaging and painful results of childhood trauma is that we develop a belief that there is something wrong with *us* rather than that there is something wrong with the situation in which we are being raised. So we deny the reality of what we are experiencing.

Denying that anything bad is happening to us is a very effective coping strategy. Believing that those around us are good, and dismissing the harm they are doing to us, can actually be an essential survival tool. As a child, facing the idea that those who care for us are not safe people to be around is simply too psychologically challenging. If a child were to recognise this they would probably fall to pieces and be unable to endure the situation in which they found themselves.

So children deny how bad the situation is. Yet they have to make sense of what is happening somehow – they know something is wrong, and they need to have a way to understand it. In the end, for most children, the only 'logical' conclusion they can come to is that they themselves are to blame. *They* must be bad, or wrong in some way, and thus they deserve what is happening to them, or they are somehow causing the situation through something that they are getting wrong.

Such beliefs can serve a child well as they struggle to cope with a terrifying situation. However, there is a payoff for this, in that the child now starts to carry a sense of shame within them: a deep shame that there is something bad or wrong about them that they can do nothing to change. This sense of shame persists into adulthood and can significantly dampen and limit the vibrancy and richness of life.

Denial of our trauma can be one of the greatest barriers to healing. In Healing The Shadow we believe it is likely that almost everyone in our society has experienced trauma, although very few people speak openly about this. As practitioners we ourselves have all experienced trauma, and we've all worked with this over the years and are on our own paths to healing. We think it is helpful for our clients to know that we have been on this journey before them. Whilst we would never share any details of our personal journey, it can be reassuring for clients to know that we have travelled this path ourselves. This is very permission-giving and is one of the reasons we can hold such a welcoming and non-shaming place for the people who seek our support.

A second, closely related, barrier to personal work is the natural desire we all seem to have to try to grade our trauma in comparison to others. Ultimately this is simply another survival strategy that children adopt when they are struggling emotionally: they tell themselves that there are others so much worse off than they are and that they really shouldn't be complaining. This helps them to have a positive attitude and to get through what they are experiencing. However, when as adults we find ourselves struggling with the ongoing effects of childhood trauma, this way of thinking can block us from seeking support, as we tell ourselves that others had it so much worse and we shouldn't complain, we shouldn't waste anyone's time.

In Healing The Shadow we don't believe that there is any objective measure of trauma. The level of trauma does not relate to any external observations of severity or timescale or type of trauma. Such comparisons are unhelpful and inaccurate.

We believe that trauma occurs in response to a distressing event or events that are so extreme or intense that they overwhelm our ability to cope, resulting in lasting negative impact. In times of fear our body has three main responses – fight, flight or freeze. All these are animal instincts – immediate short-term reactions that help us to survive life-threatening experiences. However, trauma occurs when there is an extreme type of freeze response which continues for an extended period of time with no opportunity for the original frightening event to be processed. This happens when we experience a situation we find terrifying and we are unable to react with fight or flight responses. We then become stuck in an extended 'freeze' state, unable to take in and process the intensity of what we have experienced.

Many traumas are not detectable to the outside observer. Situations that look unremarkable and benign to others can be devastating to the emotional world of a child. It is the level of fear the child experiences, along with the lack of support and the lack of ability to change the situation, that creates the trauma, not observable external factors.

Trauma occurs when we are in terror and fear for our lives. This may be clearly observable in the case of physical or sexual abuse, for example, and other forms of overt abuse. However, as children our lives completely depend on the presence, love and care of our parents. So instances of emotional abuse, abandonment or neglect are also experienced by the child as life-threatening situations, and result in the same feelings of terror and fear for our lives.

Spending your first days or weeks in an incubator, being left to cry yourself to sleep, having a mother with postnatal depression, being sent to boarding school or being sent away from home for other reasons, a parent leaving the family home, being born into a family overwhelmed with grief, having a parent overwhelmed with work, and many other relatively commonplace situations can all be extremely traumatic for the child, as they experience the terror of abandonment without any way to change or leave the situation.

Daniel Mackler, a psychotherapist who writes about the causes, consequences and significance of childhood trauma, has this to say: 'I view the norm in our culture as being highly traumatised and I view the average, and even above-average, childhood as being extremely traumatic.'[8]

In Healing The Shadow we tend to be in agreement with this statement, dramatic though it may sound. We find it the most helpful and non-shaming approach to take with our clients: to hold the view that we all carry trauma and that we all need support at some time in our lives to heal from these experiences and to integrate the parts of us that were disowned as a result of these traumas.

We find that most, if not all, of people's limiting or dysfunctional behaviours and patterns – addictions, eating disorders, depression, irrational or extreme reactions – are ways of avoiding the pain of the trauma they carry. As well as this, we see panic attacks, chronic anxiety and 'being triggered' as forms of flashback to traumatic events, where we again experience in our body all the fear and the intense feelings that overtook us back when we were first experiencing the trauma.

If a child experiences a traumatic event and is then able to release the fear, anger and grief of the experience immediately afterwards, they are less likely to suffer long-term psychological damage. However, if the child is not able to express the powerful emotions associated with the traumatic event, all the terrifying feelings get 'frozen' in their body and they are left 'traumatised' and experience long-term psychological difficulties.

Trauma theory is described in more detail in the Feeling Body (Chapter 8). We often explain these ideas to our clients so that they can gain some understanding of what is happening to them. Clients find that an understanding of the idea of trauma living in their body is extremely helpful, and this insight is often an important step in their healing journey.

Despite all the amazing advancements in the field of trauma theory, there is still a prevailing attitude amongst the general public that suffering from trauma is stigmatising and shaming. In a way this is almost inevitable because of the shame that most of us carry around our trauma. As described above, the belief that we are to blame is an integral part of many traumatic experiences. We believe that we did something terribly wrong or that we *are* wrong or bad in some way. These beliefs induce deep shame in us, so in this way shame is intrinsically linked with nearly all traumatic childhood experiences.

If, as Daniel Mackler claims, most people have experienced trauma at some time in their childhood, then it follows that most people carry this belief inside them that they are bad in some way, and they shame themselves for who they are and they deny their trauma. This means that people who haven't done deep healing work around their trauma will be unable to accept the frightened and traumatised parts inside themselves.

A general pattern we are aware of in shadow work is that people cannot accept certain aspects in others unless they can accept these same aspects within themselves. It therefore follows that people who reject the traumatised aspects of themselves will reject these aspects when they see them in others. So most people instinctively shame and belittle others whom they see as carrying trauma, as a defence against having to recognise that this is also true for themselves. The result of this large-scale shaming and rejection is that, as a society, we operate largely in denial of our collective trauma.

In Healing The Shadow we work to normalise trauma, and the understanding and welcoming of trauma is at the heart of our practice. Of course, clients who come to us may not choose to name or talk about trauma – their work may take an entirely different path. However, if and when they wish to explore traumatic events in their lives, we are prepared and able to hold them with deep understanding as fellow human beings on a similar path.

This is why we refer to Healing The Shadow as a trauma-centric practice. We believe in talking openly about trauma with our clients so that we can bring it out of shadow and it can be discussed and normalised in the context of us all having been traumatised in some way throughout our lives.

The four healing strands for trauma

In a Healing The Shadow session the client chooses their own pathway towards healing, and their practitioner trusts that the work will unfold in the way that is right for them and at the pace that is right for them. In our theoretical approach, we see four core experiences that play an important role on the path to healing trauma. Each one of the four experiences lies in a different archetypal sphere. We find that clients naturally choose these processes when the time is right for them and when they have the psychological strength they need in order to undertake this work.

As described above, trauma gets trapped in our bodies when we are in extreme fear and we have no support and no means of standing up for ourselves or escaping. So to heal from trauma we need to experience both support and protection: these are the first two core experiences that are necessary. This is what Joe naturally chose for himself when he was working with the traumatic memories of living with his stepdad. Firstly he chose protection and defence from the firefighter, then support from Ava.

We also know that most of the time children blame themselves for traumatic events and think they caused what happened by being wrong or bad in some way. So the third experience that is necessary is to start to reframe this belief: to begin to see that they did nothing wrong, that their experiences were due to external circumstances and were not caused by them, and to know they were innocent in everything that happened.

Along with this it is important to get to know the parts of ourselves that we came to believe were bad in some way. These parts need to be owned and integrated so that we can start to have acceptance and compassion for ourselves, rather than experiencing a battle inside where some parts are shunned and rejected and labelled as 'bad'.

Finally we also need to understand that the overwhelming feelings we experience in our adult life when we are overcome with emotion are not necessarily relevant to the situation that has triggered them. We need to 'unhook' this belief and to understand that these may be emotions that come from way back in our lives that now live in our body and are resurfacing.

Once we understand this we then need to learn how to manage these overwhelming emotions that are trapped in our body as a result of the traumatic experience. We need to learn that we are not going mad, nor are we going to die – we are simply experiencing very strong emotions. We need to learn how to allow these to flow in our body rather than trying to push them away, and how we can hold and be with these emotions in ourselves so that they don't overwhelm us and we are not held to ransom by them.

In summary, we see trauma through the lens of each of the four archetypes: support is given by the Heart Centred Leader, protection comes from the Action Taker, insight and understanding are gained through the Transformer and releasing emotion happens when we are in our Feeling Body. We find that working with all four archetypes in this way provides a thorough and complete model for healing from trauma. Of course, these different aspects of healing may take place in any order. There is no linear route to healing trauma, and certain areas may be revisited many times throughout the healing journey.

The Heart Centred Leader – creating psychological safety

Looking through the lens of the Heart Centred Leader archetype, we see the lack of support, care and understanding the child received. Before we can heal from trauma, we need to experience a loving, accepting and understanding attitude towards what we went through and the challenges we face as a result of this. Our past and the wounds we carry need to be seen through the lens of acceptance, love and understanding, or we will never have the confidence to turn and face what we need to face, nor will we have the self-compassion to believe we are worthy of attention and healing.

Initially this compassion needs to be modelled by others, and for many of us therapy is the first time when someone looks at us in this way, with loving eyes. We need to receive this care from someone else first before we can give it to ourselves, as we only learn to love and care for ourselves by experiencing this from others. If everything goes well in our childhood, our parents and other adults around us will model this for us. We will then internalise this and naturally love and care for ourselves – we will develop a strong Heart Centred Leader. However, trauma does not usually happen as an isolated incident – it generally happens against a backdrop of a lack of readily available and appropriate care and support for the child. If we had parents who were unwilling or unable to give us the acceptance and care we needed, then we will not have developed the ability to love and support ourselves through our trauma, and this needs to be learnt as part of the healing process.

So by having this care modelled in a therapeutic setting, we can learn to bring love and care towards ourselves and we can start to grow parts that will speak kindly to us and be accepting, compassionate and understanding towards all aspects of us. This self-compassion is an essential step towards healing our trauma.

The Action Taker – coming out of freeze

Looking through the lens of the Action Taker archetype, we see that as a child we were unable to do anything to protect ourselves or to get out of the situation we were in. When we are children we have no real power, as we are physically and emotionally unable to survive alone. We are dependent on those around us. If we experience frightening or upsetting situations and we are not able to speak up or to make any kind of difference to what is happening to us, then we can develop a sense of helplessness, and this can continue into our adult lives. It becomes an imprint that we carry within us in our inner world, a pattern of experiencing trauma and being utterly unable to help or protect ourselves. So to heal this Action Taker wound, we need to learn that now, in adult life, we *can* take action and that we can protect ourselves, set our boundaries and make a difference to our fate. This is where anger work is so essential. This is fully embodied work, where we can experience, perhaps for the first time, a sense of our own power and agency flowing around our body. This opens a doorway for us into this side of ourselves. It can bring us out of 'freeze' and into a fully embodied experience of our adult self.

The Transformer – letting go of beliefs we took on about ourselves

Looking through the lens of the Transformer archetype, we can see that we have taken on some beliefs about ourselves and the world around us that need to change in order for us to be psychologically well and whole. We need to reframe what happened, and to see the truth that we aren't to blame for what happened to us and that we are not bad in any way.

The belief that we are bad or wrong is so painful to us because it is untrue. If we really were bad, there would be no dissonance in us when we believed that. However, the truth is we never were 'bad'. No child 'deserves' to experience trauma. The world doesn't work like that. Children experience trauma due to circumstances completely out of their control. Yet many people develop beliefs that they somehow caused their childhood experiences: 'I was ugly.' 'I was too naughty.' 'I was too needy.' 'I didn't help my mum enough.' 'I was disgusting and dirty.' 'I was unlovable' and so on. These painful beliefs get carried into adulthood, unquestioned by us, and they become part of the way we see ourselves and the world.

These beliefs need to be carefully dismantled if we are to understand that we were never to blame. Letting go of such beliefs can be psychologically challenging work. If we let go of the idea that we were to blame, then it could lead to us seeing that the people whom we loved let us down badly and made poor decisions on our behalf, or that they weren't there when we needed them. However painful this process may be, it is an essential step on the path towards wholeness, as we need to put down our belief that things were our fault so that we can stop attacking ourselves. It allows the internal battle to end, and we can feel more at peace.

We can then start to reclaim these aspects that we previously saw as 'bad': 'I wasn't too needy, I was just a loving affectionate child.' 'I wasn't dirty, I was just a normal child exploring and enjoying my body.' 'I wasn't naughty, I was inquisitive and adventurous and good fun to be around.' This 'reframing' can allow us to reclaim resources and gifts and strengths in ourselves that we have locked away for many years. Discovering this gold inside us is the hidden gift in our trauma journey – we begin to find we can enjoy life in a way we never before thought possible, and we can come to love and value all parts of ourselves.

The Feeling Body – allowing the emotions to flow

Looking through the lens of the Feeling Body archetype, we see that trauma affects, and is held in, every living cell of the body. To heal this we need to come to know these sensations that are stored up in our bodies. We need to learn to feel safe with them and to allow them to flow naturally and to eventually be released from our system. We need to learn to hold ourselves through the experience of these sensations, allowing space for them in our bodies and allowing them to flow so that they are no longer trapped within us.

Feeling these feelings fully can be overwhelming. They often include a sense that we are going mad, or going to die, or both. A confident practitioner is able to support their client through holding this experience in their body and to help them understand that these feelings are from the past – they are *not* going to die *nor* are they going to go mad. As we become familiar with allowing these feelings to flow in our body, they become less terrifying and overwhelming, and we can find ways to manage them so they don't have such a detrimental impact on our lives. In addition to the work we do at Healing The Shadow, specialised somatic practices can be very helpful in learning how to hold and work with trauma in the body.

Hasani's journey

As Hasani continued with his Healing The Shadow sessions, stepping into and exploring different parts of himself each week, more and more memories of his time at boarding school emerged. Hasani had been a 'success' at his boarding school. He was academically gifted and excelled at cricket and chess. He had a group of close friends whom he did everything with, and he was grateful for the opportunities that such a good education had afforded him.

However, as he explored the feelings of different parts of himself, he discovered a part that had felt absolute terror on the first day of school. He recalled watching his parents' car drive away and feeling utter panic and disbelief at his situation.

Later he discovered a part of himself that was full of rage at having been sent away – he felt particularly angry at his mother for abandoning him in this way. He also discovered a part of himself that believed he had not been warm and loving enough and this was why his parents had chosen to send him away. He had been quite a 'bookish' child and spent a lot of time in his room, whereas his younger siblings were more playful and, in his eyes, more lovable. So he started to believe he was somehow cold and unlovable and that was why his parents chose to send him away.

He felt he had been 'spoiling' the family in some way, that he didn't belong and had to be removed. This belief persisted into adulthood.

Hasani remembered, on the first day of school, looking around for somewhere safe to go, looking for someone to talk to so that he could explain that there had been a mistake and he needed to go back home with his parents. But he found no one. He was lost in the large playground, surrounded by others who were taking no notice of him. He went to his room and cried – and cried and cried and cried. Eventually an older boy came in who had heard the noise. 'You can't cry here,' he said. 'You'll have to toughen up. No one's coming back for you – you're on your own now.'

From that moment onward Hasani put his fear and sadness aside. He realised it was not safe to show these emotions and he was going to have to hide them away if he was to survive. In that moment, he cut off the childlike parts of himself and hid them away. He put on a mask of being OK. He worked hard to please the school masters, and he was polite and friendly to avoid any trouble with his peers. He formed close friendships with a group of intelligent, thoughtful boys. However, he didn't share any of his true feelings with them. The friendships were about survival, rather than about support and care. He had learnt quickly that these were not available to him.

Hasani stopped going home in the holidays. After a few visits where he was torn with grief on having to return, he decided to save himself this torture, saying he preferred to stay and work through the holidays, when he could focus clearly on his studies and gain better grades.

The ways Hasani took on to cope with the situation he found himself in were life-saving. If he hadn't adopted these strategies, he would never have been able to survive psychologically. The drawback came, however, in adult life, when Hasani found himself unable to function emotionally and crippled with depression. The problem with hiding his sadness, fear and anger whilst at school was that he didn't only hide these powerful feelings from others – he also hid them from himself. His belief was, as he said at the start of this chapter, 'I had a happy childhood.'

Hasani had put these 'child' parts of himself into shadow. When we put parts of ourselves into shadow, we hide them away from ourselves as well as from others. Hasani suppressed all of his fear, his rage and his grief. He never felt these emotions and had completely lost touch with any memory of the trauma of his first day at school. He had no one to talk to about these feelings and he couldn't do anything to change his situation for himself, so these feelings became locked away and frozen inside him.

Unfortunately, when we put such strong emotions into shadow, we cut off large parts of our life force and vitality. So in adulthood Hasani felt a deadness inside, a lack of motivation, a lack of connection with anyone around him and a coldness inside, a kind of despair that he couldn't understand or name. Doctors diagnosed him with depression and prescribed him antidepressants, but he found they didn't really help. He managed life by working hard and hiding himself away outside of work, playing computer games and spending a lot of time online.

When he found a partner, things began to change. He found that with Simon some of his difficult feelings started breaking through. He was shocked to find himself exploding in anger at seemingly insignificant comments, and feeling so much fear when Simon travelled away for work. He found it hard to believe that Simon really loved him, and at times he would push him away and disconnect. These challenges in his relationship are what brought him to shadow work.

In his fifth session Hasani wanted to bring in support for the little seven-year-old boy on his first day at school. He brought in a loving ideal older brother, who listened to how he felt and let him cry. He said he would always be there for him, every evening after lights out, and he would listen all about his day, and he would cuddle him to sleep. This older brother understood exactly what Hasani was going through, and he cared deeply about him and the pain he was experiencing.

In the next session Hasani spoke to representations of his parents and expressed his anger at being sent away. He told them about the pain he had suffered and how angry he was that they hadn't listened the first few times he went home, when he had tried to explain how much he didn't want to go back. They had ignored his tears and told him he'd get used to it.

Hasani spent time with his practitioner stepping into the seven-year-old part of himself and talking about how he felt. He stepped back into these memories and explored them with his practitioner's loving presence and care. He shook with fear and cried many tears. The trauma began to 'unfreeze' and to become a part of him that he knew and talked about more openly. He explained to Simon about how frightened he felt when he went away for work. He no longer hid these deep feelings – he had access to them now, so he was able to deepen his relationship by sharing what was really going on for him.

In another session Hasani stepped into his power as he stood up to the messages he had received from his parents:

You're not wanted.

There's something wrong with you.

You're not part of this family.

If you love us all you will go quietly and not make a fuss.

He did anger work with these messages, using his power with the bat and the cushion to force these messages out of his inner world, refusing to accept these things anymore. He stepped into a powerful adult part of himself that was fully on his side and able to stand up for him and protect him.

Of course, his parents had never intended to give Hasani these messages. They loved him and would be horrified to know that he had suffered so much because of their decision. These were things Hasani had started to believe as he tried to make sense of his parents' behaviour. Eventually, after many difficult conversations with his parents, he started to understand their real motivations for sending him away to school: tradition on his father's side – his father had been to the same school, as had his grandfather – and inability to cope on his mother's side – his mother was overwhelmed herself at times by depression and wanted Hasani to have exciting opportunities that she felt she couldn't offer him. His relationship with his parents became very uncomfortable as he tried to process the extent of his suffering as a child. However, from his conversations with them and the Healing The Shadow work he undertook, he was eventually able to let go of the belief that he was cold and unlovable, and to see himself as someone worthy of love and affection who should never have been abandoned in the way he was. He was then, over time, able to see the genuine love that his partner, Simon, had for him, and slowly their relationship deepened as Hasani was able to trust this and let it in.

13.

A New Paradigm

Having reached this chapter, you will hopefully have gained a sense of the radical new nature of the work we do in Healing The Shadow. Our work offers a fundamentally different approach to traditional psychotherapy, and the way our sessions look and feel is quite unlike any traditional psychotherapy session.

A paradigm shift

At this time of great change in our world, many people are questioning the status quo in all areas of life and are looking for new ways forward. People are looking anew at the institutions that have been in place, largely unquestioned, for centuries, and they are looking for different ways of doing things. This is as true in psychotherapy as in any other system. We can see that many of the new ideas we use in Healing The Shadow are already taking hold in certain sections of the psychotherapeutic community – parts work, embodied work, process work and, most importantly, an understanding of the shadow.

However, whilst many people are questioning the structures and methodology of traditional psychotherapy, no comprehensive new framework has yet emerged to take its place.

We believe Healing The Shadow is a full and complete psychotherapeutic framework that represents a move into a new paradigm. That is, it offers a fundamental change in approach and underlying assumptions, meaning that the usual and accepted way of doing or thinking about psychotherapy is replaced by significantly different beliefs and practices. Healing The Shadow provides an exciting way forward and is grounded in a rigorous theoretical and ethical framework that holds the work safely and provides a powerful, effective, rewarding and sustainable therapeutic practice.

The full details of our work are outside the scope of this book; however, this chapter describes some of the beliefs we hold and some of the practices we use that represent this paradigm shift. Whilst none of these is completely new and many have been around for a long time, we believe that, taken as a whole, the beliefs and practices outlined in this chapter, along with our theoretical framework and ethical code, offer a new and complete philosophy that represents a move into a new paradigm for psychotherapy.

Whilst the most obvious differences might show up in the way the work is carried out in the practice room, just as significant, and perhaps even more of a fundamental shift, are the differences that lie in the training structure, the way practitioners are assessed and the way they are supported post-qualification.

This chapter is split into three sections: the first lists the differences in the way we practise with clients, the second outlines the differences in the way we train our practitioners, and the third describes the differences in the way we support our practitioners post-qualification.

A new paradigm for therapeutic work

Below I have listed a few of the key aspects of the way we practise in Healing The Shadow in order to highlight the differences between the way we work and traditional counselling and psychotherapy practices:

- The work is embodied and experiential. Clients inhabit and talk from the different parts of themselves, as well as talking with the practitioner about themselves and their lives.

- Session length is between two and five hours long. A minimum of two hours allows the client time to settle into the space and connect with why they are there and what they are bringing. It also allows time for the work to be brought safely to a close at the end of each session.

- Clients choose the length of session they wish to have each time. This gives the client autonomy over their own healing.

- The client chooses how long they continue to have sessions. They can stop and start whenever they wish. This ensures the client is working to their own agenda and timetable.

- We hold a clearly stated belief that the client knows what is best for themselves regarding their own life and their healing. This demonstrates the practitioner's understanding that within them the client has a competent and capable part that is able to make their own choices and decisions.

ⓥ At the start of every session the direction of the work is explicitly chosen by the client. This allows the client the opportunity to reflect on what they really want from the session and ensures that the practitioner is following the client's agenda.

ⓥ The client directs the session at every step. Nothing happens without the client's understanding and agreement. This ensures the client feels in control of the session and is free to make the decisions that are best for them.

ⓥ The client is given time to choose how to end the session. This ensures the client feels in control right up to the end of the session. They are made aware of how much time is left and can make choices around how to use that time so they can end the session in the best way for themselves.

ⓥ The practitioner shares their therapeutic ideas and beliefs openly with the client. The theoretical framework used relates clearly and directly to the work done in the room and is easy to understand. This ensures the client understands and is fully engaged with the therapeutic approach being used and that they have full ownership of their healing process.

ⓥ The theoretical framework we use is one of wholeness. We believe in the inherent wholeness of the client and in their ability to reclaim all parts of themselves and to live a full and rich life. This ensures that practitioners do not limit their clients in their growth but allow space for their transformation and expansion.

⊚ There are four strands to our work which combine to provide deep healing. These four strands weave together throughout the session and ensure the work is safe and fully integrated. They are:

1. The relationship between the client and the practitioner and the discussions they have about the client and their life.

2. The work that takes place on the carpet, with the client stepping into parts and embodying them fully.

3. The client stepping back into 'the whole of themselves' to view what has happened on the carpet and to discuss this with the practitioner, reflecting on the picture that is unfolding in front of them.

4. The client making a conscious and deliberate choice to undertake process work in order to change the patterns that are represented on the carpet.

A new paradigm for practitioner training

In Healing The Shadow we believe that the way we train practitioners needs to mirror the way we wish practitioners to run their therapeutic sessions once they are qualified. We aim to model to trainees the same ethos we wish them to bring to their clients. Rather than an attitude of 'do as I say', we work with an attitude of 'do as I do'.

Ours in an intensive two-year training and we select people whom we believe have the level of maturity and personal development necessary to reach the standard of qualified practitioner within the two-year time frame. This does not necessarily mean we require applicants to have any formal qualifications or prior professional experience. We make a judgement based on their personal qualities and their capacity to acknowledge their shadows and be authentically present with others. We find the applicant's own life experience and healing journey to be more significant than any formal qualifications or professional roles they may hold.

Having gained a place on the training and been deemed to have the necessary internal resources and maturity to embark on this journey, our trainees are welcomed wholeheartedly into the training space. They are welcomed exactly as they are: with all their flaws, wounds and shadows, as well as their gifts, strengths and competencies. We take a very small number of students each year so that they can each have personal attention and guidance and can benefit from the trainers' personal interest and investment in them. Our trainees' personal development and wellbeing matters to us as much as their professional development.

In Healing The Shadow we believe the learning process is non-linear and that learning takes place best in a therapeutic environment where all parts of the trainee are welcome and no 'performance' is required of them. This way the trainees' challenges and struggles can show themselves openly and can be worked with and healed, rather than going into shadow for fear of being shamed or judged. Acceptance of the trainee exactly as they are, and the welcoming of all the different parts of them, allows them to grow and develop in the most integrated and fulsome way possible.

The majority of the work we do on the training is experiential. Trainees immerse themselves in the theory and concepts taught in a first-hand, embodied way. The training is a therapeutic environment where each trainee can explore and grow according to their own learning style and personality type. They have full choice over what they do and don't take part in. Much of the time trainees are facilitating their peers or being facilitated by them: involving themselves deeply in the work and learning as much from being in the client place as from being in the practitioner role.

We believe trainees' personal work is vital to their training. Trainees need to experience the processes we use from a client place before going on to use them as a practitioner. This gives them an inside understanding of the client experience and they gain insight into what is needed to facilitate the process safely and effectively. However, even more importantly than this, whilst undertaking these processes trainees come to know, understand and integrate their shadows, which might otherwise impact on their effectiveness and safety as a practitioner.

We work on trainees' understanding and healing of their own shadows so that they can take awareness of these into their practice and not be overcome by unconscious behaviours. This work also allows trainees to gain an understanding of the gold that is hidden in their shadows and the unique gifts they have to offer their clients.

We work hard to ensure that trainees and trainers have high-quality adult-to-adult relationships. Space and time are given over to building these relationships, as well as to building the relationships between trainees. A powerful communication framework is used to work on relationships within the organisation and to keep them vibrant, clean, resilient and supportive. This includes a facilitated process we call the Restoring Connection process, which is used to explore any difficulties or breaches in connection between any members of the organisation. This process deepens relationships and creates a high level of trust within our community.

In Healing The Shadow our priorities are different from those of traditional accrediting bodies. We spend a high percentage of our time working on the trainees' own personal development and the exploration and healing of their shadows. We believe learning is a complex and personal process, and we give trainees a lot of choice as to how they wish to access the learning so that they can grow and develop in the way that is most effective for them.

We enjoy the freedom of teaching in this way, and we find it creates richness and vibrancy in the training experience and allows us to give attention to the work that we believe creates the safest and most competent practitioners.

We have no written essays or examinations in our assessment process. Our assessment is based on videoed sessions with clients, which are reviewed by both trainer and trainee and discussed in depth. Theory is assessed through talks trainees prepare and deliver to their peers over the final year of the training. Trainees further deepen their understanding of each subject area through listening to their peers' talks and taking part in the discussions that ensue. These discussions dive into more complex questions about the topic presented, and this engenders deeper learning for everyone involved.

In the final year, we believe it is important that trainees receive input and support around setting up and building their practice. We devote a significant amount of training time to teaching trainees about this, and to discussing the practical and emotional demands of running a practice. We explore in depth the dynamics that can play out between client and practitioner and what is necessary to keep these relationships healthy and therapeutic.

A new paradigm for practitioners post-qualifying

Having grown quality practitioners who have a high level of maturity, we then trust, support and continue to invest in these practitioners as they go out into the world post-qualification. At Healing The Shadow we have a policy of *investing* in our practitioners rather than testing them. We have an informal third year of training, which involves high levels of supervision and continuing professional development (CPD) to support the trainees in establishing their practices and overcoming the initial hurdles involved in this.

Following this informal third year, our CPD specifications require practitioners to continue to do their own personal work and also to have high levels of supervision to support them in their practice. As part of their ongoing CPD, practitioners continue to be part of the Healing The Shadow community, having regular peer supervision, assisting in running workshops, being involved in future training cohorts and creating and sharing resources and ideas.

Over the training, we invest time in creating strong bonds between practitioners so that they can go on and support each other informally as well as formally once they start their practices. The trainees get to know each other in depth: their competencies as well as their shadows. A high level of trust develops between trainees, meaning they are able to reach out and share their vulnerabilities with each other. This means that once qualified, trainees can benefit from the ongoing experience of being part of a community where they are personally known and supported and where they can continue to develop and grow.

As well as gaining support and confidence from the community, our practitioners can trust in the high level of personal and interpersonal maturity they develop during their training. This maturity means they can trust in themselves and their capacity to hold and manage the variety of different situations they may encounter as practitioners. It gives a sense of strength and safety to their work.

The work we teach has a detailed theoretical framework and clear processes and structures which support the practitioner. There is a safety in this Healing The Shadow framework which allows practitioners to feel relaxed and confident as they work. They are not required to take on a debilitating amount of responsibility for the client, since the work is guided by the client themselves and there are procedures the practitioner can rely on to support their client in working through almost any situation which arises. This, alongside the personal qualities of the practitioner, their personal maturity and their ability to hold themselves and others, makes the work inherently safe.

Our practitioners can trust in themselves, their support network and the structure and framework they are working within, and this enables them to practise with confidence.

I believe an explicit encouragement and welcome is necessary for therapists to continue to share and explore their wounds and shadow sides post-qualifying. Many therapists feel the pressure to be perfect or fully healed in order to be 'higher than' their clients. This is part of the old paradigm and may stem from the traditional doctor–patient mentality.

This pressure to be perfect can come from clients too, who may want their therapist to rescue them or be superhuman in some way. It can be easy for therapists to fall into a God complex, or a saviour complex, where they inflate themselves to fulfil the needs of their clients and deny or ignore their own wounds and limitations, hiding these away into shadow. This can be a very alluring idea. It is tempting to believe we are 'cured', fully healed or in some other way superior to our clients, as this then means we don't have to continue to face painful parts of ourselves.

However, if we try to maintain this stance of perfection, we will become brittle and highly defended. We may also become resentful, and our work can lose its joy. We are likely to become highly vulnerable to criticism and, ultimately, we will dry up, as our personal growth is stifled by this lack of humility.

So it is important that practitioners are invited to continue to bring all parts of themselves to their colleagues and supervisors and to continue to grow. This means their practice is constantly alive and vital, as their own growth process continues alongside the work they do with clients. This also increases the practitioner's compassion and humility, which are essential qualities in a therapeutic practitioner.

In the same way that practitioners need to recognise and welcome the client as a fellow human being, we also need to recognise and welcome ourselves as fellow clients. It is important to recognise that we too need to grow and heal, that we have a right to support and care and a right to set our boundaries and look after ourselves so that we can live a full and rich life. There is a principle here that I believe is very important; this is the Enfoldment Principle that was mentioned briefly in Chapter 11. Simply put, it is the belief that the capacity of the practitioner to support their client in their journey towards wellness is directly related to the practitioner's own journey towards wellness, which in itself is directly related to the support the practitioner receives from the people in their life and the institutions in which they work.

When all this is in place, we find practitioners are joyful in their work and feel well supported. They have humility and show a continued desire and interest in working on themselves. They are confident, assured, warm, open and undefended, and able to work with their clients at the deepest level.

Next steps

If you've enjoyed this book I would be grateful if you would take the time to leave a review on Amazon.

If you would like to find out more about our work at Healing The Shadow, please visit our website: htsorganisation.co.uk.

If you'd like to see our work in action, we have made a thirty-minute film which follows a client through a session and contains comments from other clients about their work with us. You can find this film on the home page of our website.

If you've enjoyed this book and would like to experience sessions with a qualified Healing The Shadow practitioner, then please do get in touch. Any of our practitioners will be happy to speak with you and to have a discussion about what you are looking for and whether this work might be the right next step for you. You can find details of all our qualified practitioners on our website.

Indeed, you may even be interested in training with us on our intensive two-year practitioner training programme, in which case we'd love to hear from you. Again, you can find further details of the training and the application process on our website.

Please note: a prerequisite for applying for our training is to have at least fifteen hours' experience of working with a Healing The Shadow practitioner.

Suggested Reading

The shadow

A Little Book on the Human Shadow, Robert Bly, 1988

Owning Your Own Shadow: Understanding the Dark Side of the Psyche, Robert A. Johnson, 1994

Meeting the Shadow: The Hidden Power of the Dark Side of Human Nature, Connie Zweig and Jeremiah Abrams, eds, 1990

The Dark Side of the Light Chasers: Reclaiming Your Power, Creativity, Brilliance, and Dreams, Debbie Ford, 2001

Shadows Before Dawn: Finding the Light of Self-Love Through Your Darkest Times, Teal Swan, 2015

Projection

Inner Gold: Understanding Psychological Projection, Robert A. Johnson, 2017

Parts work

Embracing Our Selves: The Voice Dialogue Manual, Hal Stone and Sidra Stone, 1998

The archetypes

Warrior, Magician, Lover, King: A Guide to the Male Archetypes Updated for the 21st Century, Rod Boothroyd, 2018

The Inner Child

A Secure Base, John Bowlby, 2005

Healing the Shame That Binds You, John Bradshaw, 2005
Home Coming: Reclaiming and Championing Your Inner Child, John Bradshaw, 1999
Why Love Matters: How Affection Shapes a Baby's Brain, Sue Gerhardt, 2014

Trauma

In an Unspoken Voice: How the Body Releases Trauma and Restores Goodness, Peter A. Levine, 2010
Waking the Tiger: Healing Trauma: The Innate Capacity to Transform Overwhelming Experiences, Peter A. Levine and A. Frederick, 1997
Unshame: Healing Trauma-Based Shame Through Psychotherapy, Carolyn Spring, 2019

The body

The Body Keeps the Score, Bessel van der Kolk, 2015
The Myth of Normal: Illness, Health and Healing in a Toxic Culture, Gabor Maté, 2024
The Language of Emotions: What Your Feelings Are Trying to Tell You, Karla McLaren, 2023
Resolving Traumatic Memories: Metaphors and Symbols in Psychotherapy, David J. Grove and B. I. Panzer, 1991
Clean Language: Revealing Metaphors and Opening Minds, Wendy Sullivan and Judy Rees, 2008

Addiction

In the Realm of Hungry Ghosts: Close Encounters with Addiction, Gabor Maté, 2018
Chasing the Scream: The First and Last Days of the War on Drugs, Johann Hari, 2016

Endnotes

1 Robert Bly, *A Little Book on the Human Shadow* (Harper San Francisco, 1988)

2 Carl Jung, 'The Structure of the Unconscious' (1916) in *Collected Works of C. G. Jung, Volume 7 – Two Essays in Analytical Psychology* (Princeton University Press, 1992)

3 A. Mehrabian and M. Wiener, 'Decoding of Inconsistent Communications', *Journal of Personality and Social Psychology* (1967) 6 (1): 109–114. doi:10.1037/h0024532. PMID 6032751; A. Mehrabian and S. F. Ferris, 'Inference of Attitudes from Nonverbal Communication in Two Channels', *Journal of Consulting Psychology* (1967) 31 (3): 248–252. doi:10.1037/h0024648. PMID 6046577

4 Peter A. Levine, *In an Unspoken Voice: How the Body Releases Trauma and Restores Goodness* (North Atlantic Books, 2010)

5 Robert Bly, *A Little Book on the Human Shadow* (Harper San Francisco, 1988)

6 David Crumm, 'The Ram Dass Interview: Smiling as He Teaches About *Polishing the Mirror*', Read the Spirit (14 July 1013), www.readthespirit.com/explore/the-ram-dass-interview-on-polishing-the-mirror-you-cant-help-but-smile-hes-still-teaching-us, accessed 14 June 2024

7 Carol Wilson, *The Work and Life of David Grove: Clean Language and Emergent Knowledge* (Troubador Publishing Ltd, 2017)

8 Daniel Mackler, Wild Truth: Healing from Childhood Trauma, www.wildtruth.net, accessed 5 June 2024

www.ingramcontent.com/pod-product-compliance
Lightning Source LLC
Chambersburg PA
CBHW031120020426
42333CB00012B/162